DAISY

INCLUDES ENLARGED VERSION
IF I WERE A WOMAN
BY T.L. **OSBORN**

BOOKS BY
DAISY AND T.L. OSBORN

FIVE CHOICES FOR WOMEN WHO WIN
GOD'S LOVE PLAN
HEALING THE SICK - A Living Classic
HOW TO BE BORN AGAIN
NEW LIFE FOR WOMEN
POWER OF POSITIVE DESIRE
RECEIVE MIRACLE HEALING
SOULWINNING — A Classic on Evangelism
THE BEST OF LIFE
THE GOOD LIFE
THE GOSPEL ACCORDING TO T.L. & DAISY
THE WOMAN BELIEVER
THERE'S PLENTY FOR YOU
WOMAN WITHOUT LIMITS
WOMEN & SELF-ESTEEM
YOU ARE GOD'S BEST

Most Osborn books and audio or video cassettes are available at quantity discounts for bulk purchases, to be used for gifts, resale, ministry outreaches, educational or other purposes.

For these and other titles, write to:
OSFO PUBLISHERS
P.O. Box 10, Tulsa, OK 74102 USA

Publisher

OSBORN FOUNDATION INT'L
Box 10 Tulsa, OK 74102 USA

Australia: Box 54, GPO, Sydney, NSW 2001 (A.R.B.N. 000 419 670)
Canada: Box 281, Adelaide St. Post Sta., Toronto M5C 2J4
England: Box 148, Birmingham B3 3EQ (A Registered Charity)

DEDICATED

To my daughter,
LaDonna Carol Osborn,
pastor of
International Gospel Center
Tulsa, Oklahoma;
To my granddaughters
LaVona Marie
Danessa Carol
Cassandra Lorae
Kimberly Dawn;
To my granddaughters-in-law,
Elisabeth Daniele
Carina Medina;
To my great granddaughters
Rachel LaVon
Madalena Altisadora
Stephanie Nicole
and
To every daughter
in the global community
of human families.

THE AUTHOR

ISBN 0-87943-090-7
Copyright 1991 by Daisy Washburn Osborn
Printed in the United States of America
All Rights Reserved

Most Osborn books and cassettes are available at quantity discounts for bulk purchase to be used for gifts, resale, ministry outreaches, educational or other purposes.

For details write:

OSFO Publishers
Box 10
Tulsa, OK 74102 USA

CONTENTS

INTRODUCTION

You Are Special

Women of God.
We've been redeemed.

Women of God,
Called, chosen, highly esteemed.

Forward in Power,
Planting good seed.

Women of God,
This is the hour,
In Jesus we're free.

These powerful words make up the theme song of my mother's ministry to women around the world. This book comes from Dr. Daisy's heart to yours, because she knows how special you are in God's plan.

* * *

Women of God ... Women are God's wonderful and unique idea. *You* are God's idea. *You* are created by God, in His image and for His good purpose. *You* are an original.

God *saw you before you were born and scheduled*

9

each day of your life before you began to breathe.[Ps.139:16 LB] His plans for you are *good ... to give you a future and a hope.*[Je.29:11 LB]

Because women are redeemed, the good news is that *we are no longer slaves* (to anything or anyone), *but God's own daughters. Everything He has belongs to us.*[Ga.4:7 LB] Just think of it! *You* are a somebody — a member of God's family now. *You* are royalty.

This book, in your hands, is evidence that *you* are ready to experience the exhilaration of real living.

God created *you* for life's *best.* Jesus makes it available to you *now.*

As an introduction to this book, there are at least ten fundamental truths which I am sharing here for the purpose of fostering and encouraging *Women And Self-Esteem.*

There is an added potential to living that is available to you as a Jesus-woman, when you embrace these 10 Gospel Basics in your life.

The demoralizing effects of outdated, religious traditions which limit women in their ministry as Christ's messengers can only be remedied by a knowledge of liberating truths.

These ten gospel truths form an unshakable foundation of faith and of self-esteem for any woman who embraces them without racial or sexual interpretation.

* * *

Gospel Basic #1:
Faith In God's Word

God's word is seed. When it is planted in a woman or in a man, it will always grow, whether you pray for it to grow or not. God established the unchanging law that a seed will reproduce itself. When you have faith in God's word and when you speak it as Jesus did, when you embrace it and plant it in the hearts of hurting people, it will reproduce itself in women the same as it will in men.

There is no basis for contact with God without the acceptance of the integrity of His word as being absolute for *you.* Both God's word and Jesus' ministry on the earth reveal ...

Gospel Basic #2:
Value Of Human Persons

Culture and religion circumscribes women in roles and categories which restrain them within prescribed social structures. Religion usually implies that people are of little value, influencing them to crawl and to cower before whatever deity they may be taught to worship.

But God sees you as a human person, His ultimate creation, the one for whom He gave *His Son* in order to redeem you back from Satan's control. Jesus was God-in-the-flesh and in encounters with people, He never saw color, race, sex, social status or physical characteristics. He saw *people* as God's creation — highly valued with divine potential, and never hopeless.

The Bible says that *God so loved the world that He gave His only begotten Son, that whoever believes in Him should not perish but have everlasting life.*Jn.3:16 *For God sent not His Son into the world to condemn the world , but that the world through Him might be saved.*Jn.3:17 This liberating truth is for you as a woman — now and it brings into focus ...

Gospel Basic #3:
Salvation Through Christ

Jesus Christ restores women and men to their Creator, their heavenly Father. He is *the Way* for God to come home to live in them again. It is through Him, not through good works or church membership or social standing, that you are saved and receive right standing with God. Jesus frees you to *become a new creature in Christ, then old things are passed away and all things become new.*2Co.5:17

Salvation through Christ means you are qualified to begin this discovery and to begin living the kind of lifestyle that God originally planned for you. This is possible through ...

Gospel Basic #4:
Love-Power, Prayer And New Life

Love is the core of your new life because *God is love,* and He has come to live in you.[2Co.6:16 LB] The life that was in Jesus is now in you. So you can do *all things through Christ who strengthens you.*[Ph.4:13 LB] Power wells up and flows through you because you recognize that *greater is He (Jesus) that is in you than he (the devil) that is in the world.*[1Jn.4:4]

You are restored to your Source again. This makes you ready for Jesus to work through you as His representative of love. The light turns on as you make the beautiful discovery of ...

Gospel Basic #5:
People — Christ's Body Today

We say it this way: *God is Spirit. You are His flesh.* Your hands and your feet become Love's hands and feet now. Your eyes and your ears become Love's eyes and ears now. This has nothing to do with your gender.

You are Love's representative now in your world of influence. You are restored to God, and in order to accomplish all that you are motivated to do, you recognize the value of and the need to utilize your God-given abilities through ...

Gospel Basic #6:
Ministry Of The Holy Spirit

The Holy Spirit gives you, as a woman, the same power that flowed through Jesus Christ to people. The Holy Spirit's purpose is to reveal Jesus to the world as *the Way, the Truth and the Life.*[Jn.14:6] He functions as your teacher who leads you into all truth,[Jn.17:17] so that *You shall know the truth, and the truth shall make you free.*[Jn.8:32]

Further revelation of Jesus in you and an ongoing unfolding of His style of living helps you to see the necessity for ...

Gospel Basic #7:
Total Healing And Miracles

Your body is the temple of the Holy Spirit,[1Co.6:19] and you realize God wants you well. He needs your body through which to reach people with the gospel of Jesus Christ.

When you are born again, you are made new in spirit, mind and body and you become *a new creature in Christ,*[2Co.5:17] with *the life of Jesus made manifest also in your mortal flesh.*[2Co.4:10] — which is physical health.

Your life takes on new value. You are a *somebody* with purpose for reaching out to others. You excitedly stretch out to incorporate into your lifestyle ...

Gospel Basic #8:
Seed-Faith And God's Best

Now you can realize the value of acquiring money. *People* are the reason for material blessings in your life, so that you can be a channel for lifting and blessing and helping them. Having money becomes an exciting and a vital part of your involvement in God's work, as a woman.

The principle of sowing and reaping makes it happen, and predetermines your tomorrow. Your own financial growth is determined by the degree to which you commit your faith and your actions to building a better world. Your future is in your hands today in the form of seed that can be planted in the fertile soil of people.

You comprehend the planting of financial seed in order to harvest more. Excitement wells up and you desire God's best in order to share more with others. Your own ministry enhances your community and inspires you to embrace ...

Gospel Basic #9:
World Missions And Evangelism

You are energized with the awareness that what is good for you is good for someone else — what works at home and in your community will work in the homes and in the communities of the world. You remember Christ's commission, and it becomes a part of your dynamic new lifestyle. He said to *go into all the world and preach the gospel to all creatures.*[Mk.16:1]

Christianity takes on a broad international field of ministry, and a world vision unfolds in your heart. You have God's perspective now, just like Jesus did, and you are confident that true fulfillment in life is wrapped up in ...

Gospel Basic #10:
Lordship Of Jesus Christ

Real living for you is anchored in the Lordship of Jesus Christ in your life as a woman.

He *is all of God in a human body.*[Col.2:9 LB] He is your life,[Jn.5:12] your love,[1Jn.4:7,8] your strength,[Ps.19:14] your hope,[1Ti.1:1] your salvation or wholeness in every way,[1Th.5:9] your gentle Master,[Mt.11:29-30] your friend.[Ro.5:10-11 LB; Ja.2:23]

Jesus Christ is your best friend and to reproduce the best in other people, you become a seed planter of His word wherever you go.[Col.1:28 LB]

* * *

These 10 Gospel Basics are what the church of Jesus Christ should be known for worldwide. As a woman, you can embrace these fundamentals, and begin to express them, right where you are, regardless of your gender.

That perspective of life and those ten fundamentals of gospel truths are what I believe produce real, dynamic, productive, healthy and happy *Women And Self-Esteem*, and that is the purpose of this book which my wonderful mother has written.

Rev. LaDonna Osborn, Pastor
Int'l Gospel Center
Tulsa, OK USA

WOMEN & SELF-ESTEEM

I

WOMAN'S
SELF-WORTH

THE PURPOSE OF this book is to encourage every girl, every young lady, every housewife, every woman to take a new look at herself — to reassess her own value, to re-examine her own abilities and to accept her unlimited potential in life — as a daughter of God, redeemed and esteemed by Jesus Christ, and restored to the place of high honor for which God created her.

Most of the world today represses female initiative, restricting them to one level or another of servitude, subordination, or outright female bondage.

In the Christian church worldwide, traditional theology has extracted two statements by Paul, out of their context, and used them to establish a doctrinal *absolute* that consistently restricts women to silence in the church and prohibits them from initiative and leadership.

The power of the Holy Spirit in a woman's life is no different than in a man's life.

Jesus came to redeem women the same as men, and to use them as His co-workers, His disciples, His messengers, His representatives —just the same as He uses men.

Let Spirit-filled women come down from their feminine pedestals and be God's women, fulfilling His dream — cost whatever it may in money or physical effort or religious opposition or persecution. Let women engage themselves in the ministry for which the Holy Spirit rests upon them — witnessing of Jesus and sharing Him with their world.

Chapter 1

WOMAN'S SELF-WORTH

Your HEAVENLY FATHER has a beautiful plan for your life — one that no one else on earth can fulfill, because you are unique. You are the only one of you that God has.

Religious tradition and Jewish custom has been relentless in its suppression of women. Even those extraordinary women who have overcome female subjugation and have launched out and have done exploits in Christ's name have had little recorded about their triumphs of faith.

Even in politics, it has only been a few decades since women gained the right to vote.

Most of the world today represses female initiative, restricting them to one level or another of servitude, subordination, or outright female bondage.

From Moslem nations where women must cover their faces and bodies with long flowing robes, to uncultured tribes where tradition relegates

21

them to a status little above animals, the role of women is one of subservience and inferiority, and it should not be.

In the Christian church worldwide, traditional theology has extracted two statements by Paul,[1Co.14:34; 1Ti.2:11-12] out of their context, and used them to establish a doctrinal *absolute* that consistently restricts women to silence in the church and prohibits them from initiative and leadership.

This message will help you discover who you really are — that in God's eyes, you are His special child — equal to anyone else in the world and designed by Him with unlimited potential.

Unlimited Ministry

My husband, T.L. Osborn, and I have spent over five decades already, proclaiming the gospel to millions — face to face — in over 70 nations.

My role as a woman has been unlimited, and yours can be too.

It has been my privilege to organize the crusades, to meet heads of state and other government officials, to secure the permits, contract the stadiums and grounds, to install the equipment, negotiate with businesses for tons of literature and purchase thousands of *Tools for Evangelism*.

I have organized the cooperating pastors, set up

the Workers' Institutes and Convert Schools and preside over the crusades. Then I alternate with my husband, teaching and preaching daily in these meetings when our crusade commences.

In addition to all of that, my responsibility as Corporate President of our OSFO International World Headquarters, places all of our overseas offices under my charge, with our enormous worldwide missionary outreaches.

Being a woman does not change me from being a believer, a disciple of Jesus Christ, His follower, His servant.

What He said to all believers, He says to me — and to you also.

His Great Commission applies to women the same as to men.

The power of the Holy Spirit in a woman's life is no different than it is in a man's life.

The Role Of God's Woman

Not long ago, I had yet another encounter with some of the traditional barriers which professional religion has set up to limit women in ministry.

I was delegated by the board of directors of OSFO International to visit an area in a certain nation which had been deprived of hearing the gospel. Church leaders in bordering districts were concerned and had appealed for our help in evangelizing another unreached area.

Researching the facts confirmed that a valid and urgent need did exist.

We were prepared to finance the opening and establishing of churches throughout the region, but the groundwork had to be done and the details worked out carefully so that the seed-idea of a great plan for God would not be aborted.

The Problem:
I Was A Woman

Upon my arrival, a church bishop, together with a delegation of pastors, met me at the airport. They had graciously prepared a *program* for me. The problem: The activities scheduled had nothing to do with the mission I was there to accomplish.

Since I believe that every problem contains the seed of its own solution, I tuned in to God for a quick discovery of the seed in this one. I certainly didn't want to offend a bishop.

Without reacting negatively to their schedule, I began to list all the things we must do before we could proceed with their program. That was just great except, all the things I had listed should, according to them, be done by a man. It would be a serious violation of their church's doctrine for me, a woman, to assume such a role of leadership.

The problem: I was a woman.

The solution: Approach this unreached area through government channels instead of through the religious hierarchy.

I was graciously accepted in my official capacity as President of OSFO International, and my being a woman did not cause even the Head of State to bat an eye.

With the cooperation and blessing of the governor, the tribal king and the village chiefs, we were able to leave no stone unturned, and the gospel invasion was carried out victoriously. My mission was accomplished, and another bishop was added to my long list of cherished clergymen friends who have accepted me in my role of leadership.

The Woman's Role
In The Fall — In Redemption

Eve, the first woman God created,[Ge.3:20] has inspired many a discourse which has resulted in ironclad church doctrines that put women *in their place,* silent and non-assertive in God's No. 1 Job.

But if a woman's disobedience resulted in the Fall of the human race, let us not forget that it was a woman's obedience that resulted in the redemption of humankind.

God chose a woman as His channel for redemption, forgiveness and eternal salvation. A woman was used to bring joy, peace, love, comfort and fulfillment to the human race.[Lu.1:26-38]

Women were active in the ministry of Jesus.[Lu.8:1-3]

The last person at the cross was a woman.[Mk.15:47]

The first person at the tomb was a woman.[Jn.20:1]

The first person to proclaim the message of the resurrection was a woman.[Mt.28:8]

The first preacher to the Jews was a woman.[Lu.2:37]

Women were at the historic prayer meeting following Christ's ascension.[Ac.1:14]

Women were in the Upper Room on the Day of Pentecost and were given power to be *witnesses* of Christ, the same as the men.[Ac.2:4;1:8]

The first persons to greet the Christian missionaries, Paul and Silas, in Europe were women.[Ac.16:13]

The first European convert was a woman.[Ac.16:14]

Are these facts important?

Do they have a message for us? Do they relate to women today? I believe they do.

26

Classic Example Of A Winning Woman

There is no better example of a *Woman's Self-Worth*, than Mary of Magdala, a demon-possessed business woman who came to Jesus, was delivered by Him, became His follower and supporter, assisted in the business arrangements, was at the cross, helped prepare His body for burial, was there when Jesus arose and was visited by Him, received His message, delivered it to the apostles, was filled with the Holy Spirit on the Day of Pentecost, and obviously was an anointed messenger and witness of Jesus Christ in the early church.

Total Deliverance

Mary Magdalene had seven demons.

Demons do terrible things to people. A beautiful individual, under the influence of evil, will commit sins otherwise unimaginable.

Remember, *The thief* (Satan) *comes only to steal, and to kill and to destroy.*[Jn.10:10] That is what demons were doing to Mary. But Jesus cast those demons from her so that she could have life, real life, eternal and abundant life.

Jesus delivers from bad habits that contaminate the body, mind and spirit, and causes us to develop habits that help to cleanse and purify ourselves as well as others. We save life instead of destroying it.

That is what Jesus did for Mary who had the seven demons. That is what He is still doing for women and men today.

A Happier Ending

In one of our crusades, three handsome young men flew for ten hours from Europe, to attend the meetings and to be blessed.

Two beautiful young prostitutes saw them in town, followed them to their hotel and made every possible attempt to lure the handsome young visitors to their rooms.

But the fellows were real Christians — involved in soulwinning ministries among the youth of Europe.

They knew how to present Christ to these girls. The result: both ladies attended the crusade, heard T.L. Osborn's message about the woman of Samaria who believed on Christ and influenced her whole village to come and see His wonders.

The girls were saved and healed. They were referred to one of the local pastors who welcomed them to church. They learned rapidly and became strong Christians and faithful members.

Later that pastor attended another crusade, with a group from his church. Those young women were among them; they had become stalwart Christians and now they have become leaders, teaching and sharing the Jesus-life with others.

Jesus Christ came to those young ladies like He came to Mary Magdalene. He delivered them like He delivered Mary. They began to follow Him like Mary did.

That is what can happen to you. You may not be possessed of seven demons, but whatever your need is, Jesus is coming to you — right now, through this message — and before you have finished reading it, your life is going to be identified with Him in a new way. You will become one of God's women with self-worth.

And what happened next to Mary Magdalene?

From Shame To A Great Name

Mary was completely delivered.

Jesus took the good in Mary — her God-given ability — and made her a useful, successful person. She became a minister to human needs. According to respected Bible commentaries, she was on Jesus' team as He went from village to village. [Lu.8:1-3]

Jesus came to redeem women the same as men, and to use them as His co-workers, His disciples, His messengers, His representatives — just the same as He used men.

29

Since Jewish religion traditionally suppressed women, writers of the Scriptures dared not make much mention of their acts of faith, but a close study of women in New Testament history clearly shows them in places of great influence and action, carrying out the new role of the new redeemed woman in the church of Jesus Christ.

There is deliverance for every woman on earth — not only deliverance from the chains and bondage of demons and sin, but deliverance from the chains and bondage of religious tradition that has sentenced her to silence and restricted her to the limits imposed by male prejudice.

When Jesus becomes Master of your life, you as a woman can do anything God puts in your heart to do. The bad is choked out by the good which God grows in you through His new life.

Woman Of Esteem On Jesus' Team

According to Bible scholars, Mary had business ability. She was actually a highly successful woman. Her madness was periodic. But in her rational times, she gained wealth through her God-given capability. But the devil tried to destroy her talent. Then Jesus came and made her into a pillar of faith in His ministry.

Dr. John Haley says in his Bible commentary that Mary Magdalene was perhaps the *leading woman of Jesus' group.* She was *one at the head of*

Jesus' religious work. She and other women went ahead of Jesus to make necessary preparations for Him and the other members of His team.

Mary was grateful for her new life and showed it by being involved with Jesus' ministry. That is a beautiful picture of *Woman's Self-Worth.*

Subdued By Chauvinism
Endued For Evangelism

I have a friend in Africa who is the wife of a prominent evangelical leader.

Until she attended one of our Women's Conferences, she was timid, non-expressive and did little more than warm a church pew.

Her husband was revolutionized by our conference. He saw how his own male superiority complex made no allowance for his wife's ministry to develop. Her potential was totally uncultivated.

As a successful leader, my friend's husband was inundated by calls to preach and minister. He drove himself day and night, almost to the breaking point, while his allegiance to archaic religious tradition kept his wife's powerful personality and energy shackled and restrained.

They both got their eyes open. He saw the terrible waste of human energy and influence that church tradition had imposed by keeping the women of his great congregation in silence.

She realized how ridiculous it was for her to allow herself to be so subdued by chauvinistic prejudice. She had actually retired within herself and had even lost her drive for winning souls to Christ.

In the conference, I preached about how Jesus delivered Mary Magdalene — not only from demons, but from the Jewish tradition that kept women as chattel and little above the animal level.

That couple was delivered — he from his religious chauvinism, and she from her docile submission to man's inbred dominance.

That African woman, with the encouragement of her revolutionized soulwinning husband, began to realize the fact that she was filled with the Holy Spirit the same as her husband; that she had the same anointing, the same faculties and the same responsibility to share Jesus with the world as her husband.

She not only became a powerful voice and influence in their rapidly growing church organization, but she began to organize the women of the area.

Today they have given birth to an African Women's Organization of preachers, evangelists, church-builders, convention-speakers, community promoters, home-builders, school and clinic-organizers. They now have built a Pan-African Women's Headquarters Building and Teaching Center. They have done it so well, that even the government is recognizing their influence and their contribution to their nation.

Be Free From Non-Assertive Silence

Mary Magdalene was completely delivered by Jesus Christ — not only from demons, but from Jewish religious male domination. And I pray that every woman who reads this will have a miracle deliverance — not only from sin, disease and negativism, but also from the tradition of churchmen that locks God's army of women in a pious world of silence — which, by the way, has been a great convenience for women who lack drive and zeal and daring courage for God's work.

After all, how convenient it is for women to excuse themselves by simply saying, *But I am a woman and I am to be silent.* It is easy to have the admiration of the male in the church as long as you are silent and non-assertive.

But never forget: Strong men never react negatively to the qualified leadership and participation of strong women.

This world is lost. The gospel must be proclaimed by every voice and instrument possible.

Christ's commission is to all believers. The Church can no longer afford the silence of two-thirds of her constituency.

Women As Disciples Of Christ

Mary Magdalene became a follower of Jesus. She was one of His disciples. She sat at His feet as a learner.

You can do the same. You learn by reading the Gospels. Make a study of Jesus' life and ministry and you will see that women are not to be sub-dued, inferior, non-expressive Christians. Women are redeemed by Christ, to be His witnesses, His disciples, the same as men. Women were very much a part of Jesus' life and ministry then, and must continue to be a vital part today.

When you read the Gospels — Matthew, Mark, Luke and John — you can make the teachings of Jesus come alive by putting your name in the scripture. Say *woman* or *she* in place of *man* and *he*. Then pray, and Jesus will talk to you.

This is the way the Jesus-woman of the Jesus church lives.

Age Not A Factor

A young girl was converted in Africa. She loved Jesus and was sensitive to His Spirit. She wanted to work for Him and to be an evangelist. But people scoffed at her. She was a girl. Girls could not preach. Girls had to become brides. They were worth a good price to their fathers who would collect a dowry for their marriage.

Day and night this girl yearned to tell others about Jesus.

One night she had a dream. She saw her crippled grandmother. She put her hands on her and the paralyzed woman was miraculously healed.

This girl got an idea from a dream, and she acted upon it. She went to her grandmother just as she had dreamed; she laid her hands on the paralyzed woman, in the name of Jesus, and the miracle took place. The woman was healed.

She realized that God had called her to minister to the needs of others. She obeyed. Soon she was preaching to hundreds, then thousands, then tens of thousands, and praying for the masses. She was just a girl, but God was using her and marvelous miracles and conversions were taking place.

What a beautiful idea God had — a teenage African village girl, preaching to multitudes and leading them to Christ.

That girl became one of God's *Women With Self-Esteem.*

Some Have Dared

Aimee Semple McPherson was a young woman from the prairies of Western Canada.

She set out to preach Christ. It was not easy. She was persecuted and criticized by theologians everywhere. She was a woman. She should not preach. She should be silent — whether souls were going to hell or not. But she had a vision. She had a call, and she paid the price to obey the call.

In religion, rules and traditions are so often given greater importance than life and deliverance.

It was not easy for Aimee Semple McPherson to load her children and their scanty belongings in an old Model-T Ford Touring Car and cross the western desert, to carry the gospel of healing and salvation to the new California frontier.

But that courageous woman reached some of the greatest crowds in the history of evangelism, and brought peace and healing miracles and salvation to multitudes of people in Christ's name.

Tens of thousands of people who were added to the churches of that epoch were brought to Christ in the great crusades which that woman so brave-ly conducted.

She was another of God's *Women With Self-Esteem.*

Ever since God poured out His Holy Spirit on the women as well as the men, He intended to use them in the same way that He uses men. But Jewish heritage and culture predominated so that Christian theological tradition has relentlessly kept women in the background, and little has ever been recorded about their faith exploits and gospel ministries.

Mary Magdalene became a follower of Jesus, an imitator of His life and ministry. He said, *As My Father has sent Me, even so send I you,*[Jn.20:21] and that includes the women.

Sowing While Growing

Mary Magdalene became a partner in her Lord's ministry.

Mary, Joanna (the wife of King Herod's business manager) and Susanna are women named in the Gospels as some of those who *contributed from their private means to the support of Jesus and His disciples.*[Lu.8:2-3 LB]

These women had been healed, delivered or otherwise blessed by Jesus' teaching and they learned to share with Jesus in ministering to the needs of others. They expressed in a material way their gratitude to Him. They made it possible for His ministry to reach more and more people.

Mary had heard and believed Jesus' message: *Give, and it shall be given to you.*[Lu.6:38] She sowed and she reaped. Mary was a giver. As a follower of Jesus, that is among the first lessons to be learned in order to enjoy a fulfilled, happy life of abundance.

There is no question in my mind but that God wants a host of Mary Magdalenes today — enterprising women who can build businesses into great successes, producing high profits so that God's No. 1 Job can be financed by them worldwide.

Use It Or Lose It

A young woman was converted in one of our Asian crusades. She had a desire to spread the gospel to others.

She studied her Bible and began sharing Jesus with people. Then she suddenly had a bright idea: Form a business and make money, then use the profits to organize and finance evangelistic projects.

Like Mary Magdalene, she used her business talent as a partnership for the ministry of Christ until, not only did she become an effective preacher, evangelist and Bible teacher herself, but her business ability also developed into a powerful tool for evangelism.

She had an idea from God: Put her business talent to work for the ministry of Christ. Make money for His work.

It was just an idea, but she acted on it and, like Mary, she became a partner with Christ — not only preaching and reaching souls herself, but building a business enterprise to finance the evangelistic outreaches she had organized. She learned the secret of growing her talents through use instead of losing them by misuse.

What an incredible thing for an Asian woman. What an affront to theological tradition in Asia. A woman preacher in Asia. But her idea worked.

And I am expecting to see armies of such women raised up all over the world, anointed by the Holy Spirit, doing God's work on every level, on a large scale.

That is the opportunity for God's *Women With Self-Esteem.*

The Unlimited Woman

Women, anointed by God's Spirit can do anything men can do. Today they chauffeur trucks and buses, operate machinery, weld steel, pilot airplanes, captain ships, direct conglomerates; women are doctors, teachers, lawyers, politicians;

women are governors, senators, judges, provincial commissioners, presidents and prime ministers of nations.

What a waste for religious tradition to shackle this enormous human resource for God and to restrict them to pious silence in God's No. 1 Job.

Let Spirit-filled women come down from their feminine pedestals and be God's women, fulfilling His dream — cost whatever it may in money or physical effort or religious opposition or persecution. Let women engage themselves in the ministry for which the Holy Spirit rests upon them — witnessing of Jesus and sharing Him with their world.

Women, like Mary Magdalene, were partners in His work then, and women are used of God to meet the needs of His work today. Jesus used human channels then — both men and women alike — and He uses human channels today.

Womankind Exonerated

Mary Magdalene proclaimed Christ's message.

The most basic message of our Christian faith is the resurrection of Jesus from the dead. Amazing as it may seem, a woman was the first person to proclaim that great news.

I believe that it is significant that Jesus trusted a woman and, in fact, ordained and commissioned her to proclaim the first message of His resurrection.

Jesus was making it very clear that the redemption of humankind at the cross had restored womanhood to her original place of equality in God's plan.

In the beginning God created humankind, male and female, equal before Him. Jesus, through His life, death and resurrection redeemed humankind — male and female, equally.

Equal Access

Women and men alike had access to God once again on an individual and equal basis, with Jesus as their mediator.

As Paul said, *We are no longer Jews or Greeks or slaves or free men or even men or women, but we are all the same. We are one in Christ Jesus.*[Ga.3:28 LB]

Women, as well as men, would now be filled and anointed with the same power of the same Holy Spirit, for the same purpose and the same ministry — to witness of Jesus Christ and to proclaim His gospel to every creature, in all the world.

What is preaching? Simply telling what you know about Jesus. When a Christian does that, and quotes some Bible verses to back up what is said, that is the greatest preaching on earth.

Mary told what Jesus had done for her and she delivered her message. That is preaching.

So, why should women not preach? If the Bible is to be accepted and obeyed by all believers, then women and men alike (all believers) are commissioned by Christ to *go into all the world, and preach the gospel to every creature.*[Mk.16:15]

In fact, in the new church that was born on the day of Pentecost, people were no longer men or women, bond or free, Jews or Gentiles, preachers or non-preachers. All are Christ's witnesses.

So often in our ministry together, my husband, T.L. Osborn, and I have had the great joy of seeing women (men too, of course) come to Christ just like Mary Magdalene did and then parallel her life-style as disciples of Jesus.

From Prostitute To Pastor

In one of our Latin American crusades, a prostitute accepted Christ. She had been a castaway, abandoned because she was dying of cancer. With no hope of life, no knowledge of true love and no faith in God, she was brought to our crusade.

She listened as we related the account of Jesus and of God's plan of redemption. She believed and accepted Him into her heart. Her eyes became a fountain of tears that bathed her face.

She said, *Oh, I feel so clean. I feel like a virgin again. That awful guilt of sin is gone. I feel so free, so light, so wonderful.*

Then she asked: *What can I do to show Jesus I love Him and am His follower?*

Every day she grew in Christ and in a few weeks that former prostitute, healed of cancer, was spending all of her time doing what we had counseled her to do, preaching and telling others about Jesus.

Then the inevitable happened. She had led many people to Christ and she felt a responsibility to help them more.

She built a large church — a soulwinning church — with thousands of members. She became a respectable pastor and leader — simply because she had never been told that a woman was not supposed to do such things.

She taught each new believer what she had learned:

1) Tell others what Jesus had done for you;

2) Quote scriptures to prove it;

3) Tell them He will do the same for them.

Will you do less?

The World Is Your Field

If the traditional church requires you, as a woman, to be silent within their walls, do not let that bother you. Go where there is a need for your message of good news. After all, most people inside the church walls have already heard of Jesus Christ.

Should you feel limited in your ministry just because you are muffled inside the institutionalized church?

The whole world is your field.

So, rather than complain about the little corners where you might be restricted, lift up your eyes and look on the fields of the whole world, where neither tradition nor Paul's restrictions apply any limits whatsoever to your ministry.

When Jesus commanded: *Go into all the world, and preach the gospel to every creature,*[Mk.16:15] that commission was for every believer, regardless of sex, color, race or culture.

With The Women

Mary Magdalene was filled with the Holy Spirit and anointed to be Christ's witness. She was at the prayer meeting in the Upper Room following the ascension of Jesus.[Ac.1:13-14]

Mary was always there. She was faithful. She

left Magdala to stay with Jesus and His other disciples. She was with Him to the end. She was at the trial in Pilate's Hall and she was at Calvary.

She was with Him at the cross. She helped prepare His body for burial. She was at the tomb. She had patience to stay when others gave up. She loved Him when others denied Him.

Mary heard Him say He would rise again. Evidently she never forgot His words. She searched for her Lord. She did not take another's word; and she resisted the doubts of others. Why? Because she had faith. She had heard Jesus teach.[Lu.1:18:31-33] Her faith had come by hearing His own words.[Ro.10:17]

Mary was there when Christ appeared near the sepulchre. Her faithfulness paid off because she heard Jesus call her by name. And she was the first one sent to announce His resurrection.

And she was there when the Holy Spirit descended. Jesus had told them *not to leave Jerusalem until the Holy Spirit came on them in fulfillment of the Father's promise.*[Ac.1:4] [LB] Mary Magdalene was there.

The Bible names the eleven disciples present among *about a hundred and twenty people with the women.*[Ac.1:15,14 TAB]

Mary was often named among the group of partners who supported and followed Jesus; and she had seen the Lord at the sepulchre and was sent by Him to tell of His resurrection. You can be sure she was one of the women present when the Holy Spirit descended.

Mary was filled with the Holy Spirit, the same as the men who were present. And her receiving this power had to be for the same purpose:

You shall be witnesses of Me to the uttermost part of the earth.[Ac.1:8]

It would be difficult for a woman to fulfill this purpose, or to *prophesy* as Peter announced that the women would do,[Ac.2:17] and remain *silent*.

Mary, therefore, became one of the truly emancipated women, God's creation, redeemed and equipped to go anywhere as His witness.

The prophecy of Joel was fulfilled.[Jl.2:28]

God began to pour out His Spirit on all flesh. *His sons and His daughters began to prophesy*, and Mary was one of them.

Supreme Esteem For Women

A new day dawned when Jesus came — for women and men alike.

We have liberty. We are no longer slaves. We are no longer bound. We have been set free. Why? Because we are loved. We are esteemed. We are needed. We are part of Jesus' church. We are members of His body. He is depending on us. The world is depending on us.

Mary Magdalene is a symbol of what Jesus came to do.

At the resurrection Christ defeated death, hell and the grave. He broke down the walls of division. He annulled the laws of segregation. He abolished the curse of racial or sexual prejudice.

In His death, burial and resurrection, He defeated Satan once and for all.

The new, liberated church was born.

The Jesus-woman for the Jesus-church emerged as a redeemed, Spirit-filled, powerful woman to fill the role for which God created and destined her.

Choose To Love

Now we have a choice. We can choose to serve, follow, obey and love our Lord. As for me, I choose Jesus and the life He offers me and every other woman and man.

How about you?

This is your moment of decision:

1. To accept Jesus in your life as your Savior and Lord; [Ro.10:9]

2. To become His follower in all things; [Mt.16:24]

3. To let Him love, serve and deliver through you; ^{Mt:25:40}

4. To become involved in soulwinning; ^{Mt.4:19}

5. To become a sower, a giver, an organizer; ^{Lu.6:38}

6. To pray earnestly and listen for His answer to you personally; ^{Mt.7:7}

7. To be filled with the Spirit so that you will have power to be His witness; ^{Ac.1:8}

8. To witness — to proclaim that Jesus is alive and *is the same yesterday, today and forever.*^{He.13:8}

Are you ready to begin this new life today?

First, this new concept had to be formed in you, and that has already happened to you through reading this message.

Now, your future, your new status, your new life of love and happiness and success and achievement and self-esteem all depend upon your willingness to make a decision right here and now, and to say to yourself and to God? From today, I will recognize *Woman's Self-Worth.*

Are you ready to do that right now? Your decision will be the key that unlocks an exciting and successful new future for you.

Pray this decisive prayer of commitment to Christ.

Prayer

O Lord, I am Your child, created in Your image, with Your breath breathed into me.

I am a channel for Your Holy Spirit to work through — an esteemed human person for Christ to live in.

I have looked up to the heavens, and I have had a new vision of myself in Your hands. I have dreamed a new dream.

I want, more than anything else in this world, to be Your instrument for good.

I am Your child, created for a unique purpose, and I am determined, from this day, to fulfill Your dream for my life.

O Lord Jesus, how marvelous to know what You did through Mary Magdalene. Do as much through me.

The demons that possessed her want to limit me too. Demons of negativism and fear, of poor self-esteem, of timidity and of inferiority, of subjection and tradition — drive them from my life forever.

Help me to discover all that I am in You, so that I can rise above these negative influences that have restricted my usefulness.

Transform my life like You did Mary Magdalene's.

Thank You that You have lifted me out of subjection and inferiority, and have put my feet on the solid road where I can become one of Your *Women With Self-Esteem*.

Thank You Lord, for finding me, like You called Mary Magdalene.

I am Your follower. I choose to share in Your ministry, to be Your partner.

I am restored. I am esteemed. I am anointed to witness to others. I receive You in my life.

From this moment, Your blood cleanses me. Your life is mine. My past is gone forever.

My weakness and inferiority, my defeat and denial of what You created me for, are gone forever.

From today, I am Your woman of esteem, fulfilling Your dream.

I am Your follower.

Thank You for Your new life.

Truly, I am born again today.

I am a new creature in Christ Jesus.

Thank You Lord.

Amen.

* * *

Now that you have taken this important step, register your decision before God right now.

As an act of faith, fill in the coupon I have included below. It will be a lasting testimony of your personal experience today.

MY DECISION

TODAY I HAVE read *Women & Self-Esteem.* I have discovered the life God created me for.

Jesus Christ, You are my Lord. I believe that you died for me — a woman, to redeem me because You esteem me.

I commit my life to do my best to please You, Lord, in all that I think and say and do. With Your grace and help, I shall share You with others.

Relying on You to help me and to keep me by Your grace, I have made this decision today in the name of my Savior and Redeemer, Jesus Christ.

Signed:_____

Date:_____

God bless you.

WOMEN & SELF-ESTEEM

II

TOTAL
FREEDOM

As A WOMAN, do not accept the submissive, silent, inferior role that you have been assigned by religion and by culture.

When you accept Jesus as Lord of your life, you have no other master. He desires to express His love and leadership through you.

The woman believer (Christian) who accepts cultural restrictions and religious restraints is limiting Jesus who craves expression through her. Only *she* can limit Christ at work in and through her life.

It takes courage for a woman to be what God created her to be. She can be a Jesus-woman if she does not fear what people say about her; if she accepts God's will and lets go of the sanctimonious patriarchal indoctrination she may have inherited.

I have seen the twins which religion gives birth to — culture and tradition. Religious women often go through life doing what they are expected to do rather than what they choose to do. They live with obligations rather than options. They bow to rules and requirements instead of enjoying the pleasure of responding to and of cultivating God's ability within them.

The Holy Spirit of God in a woman is not meant to be silent. This is good news. Believe it and live in complete freedom.

Chapter 2

TOTAL FREEDOM

T HERE IS A STORY in the gospel of Luke that
is timeless in its message. In fact, each account we
have of Jesus' encounters with people contains a
contemporary message for us. Though hidden
from the casual, indoctrinated reader, fresh, new
truth lies embedded in the Gospels, just waiting
to be discovered by a hungry, searching believer.

Jesus displayed the nature, the desire, the love
and the will of God our heavenly Father in
everything He did.[Jn.5:19; 14:9] Women can trust the
example of Jesus. Women are to emulate His
attitude and His conduct, in every situation and
in every relationship. That is the way we strive
for perfection in Christ.[Mt.5:48]

God's Character Comes Through

When Jesus walked the religious tightrope, that
is, when He taught in the synagogue or addressed very religious people, God's character of love

always came through loud and clear.

Take for example the time *Jesus was teaching in one of the synagogues on the sabbath. There was a seriously handicapped woman present who had been bent double for eighteen years and was unable to straighten herself.*

When Jesus saw her, He called her to Him and said, WOMAN, YOU ARE LOOSED from your infirmity.

And He laid His hands on her: and immediately she was made straight, and she recognized and thanked and praised God. Lu.13:10-13

Following this great demonstration of God's gentle love for women, we see a typically religious demonstration of harsh contempt for women.

But God's honesty comes through in Jesus as He replies to the ruler of the synagogue:

You hypocrite, does not each one of you on the sabbath loose your ox or your ass from the stall, and lead it away to water?

OUGHT NOT this WOMAN, being a daughter of Abraham, whom Satan has bound these eighteen years, BE LOOSED from this bond on the sabbath day? Lu.13:15-16

Sounds Of Liberation

For nearly 2,000 years those words of Jesus continue to be heard, WOMAN, YOU ARE

LOOSED — WOMAN, BE FREE! Women around the world are picking up the sound of those liberating words of Jesus and are standing up, loosed from inferiority, timidity, unworthiness and other cultural, religious bondage.

I like the way Jesus spoke to that human person in the Jewish synagogue. He indicated her original identity, the only non-cluttered name she could be called: WOMAN. With that title, there was no segregating or categorizing needed. There was no advantage in knowing if she were someone's *wife, mother, sister, neighbor,* or *friend.* There was much to be gained by the classification of *woman,* the female expression of God in whose image she was made.

Had that woman been called by any other identifying name, an immediate classification would have been made, and a cultural value established. For example, a widow had a certain value, a wife another, a mother of a son yet another, and of course the virgin daughter was rated at the top of the heap.

Regardless of your social title, your identity as a woman is your purest reflection of your heavenly Father. It is very important to remember your worth. The same price was paid to redeem you as was paid for every human person. None are inferior. All are endowed with excellence.[Jn.3:16-17]

Religious leaders or rulers have no right to

intimidate or to discriminate against you as a woman. Jesus is your only perfect example. He did not emulate religion. He was God in the flesh; divine love in a human body. He never embarrassed, frightened, threatened or discouraged women. Rather, He lifted, encouraged, befriended and reassured even the most disadvantaged person in society. *Jesus Christ is the same yesterday, and today and forever.*[He.13:8] His magnificent manner is unchanged. He sees you where you are, as you are. Your muzzle, your bridle, your obstacles and your shackles have His attention. Trust Him and He will communicate FREEDOM to you.

Woman, be free! Woman, you are loosed! These are pronouncements of your freedom by Jesus Christ.

Religious Conceit Confronted

The religious ruler in the synagogue retaliated with brazen conceit when Jesus gave the impaired woman her freedom. Can you imagine such rude treatment of a guest, anywhere except within the strict limits of pious religiosity?

Jesus knows how to relate to us, as we are, where we are. And He did a terrific job of communicating an appraisal in one single word.

The ruler waylaid the people with indignation, saying: *There are six days in which to labor: in them therefore come and be healed and not on the sabbath.* [Lu.13:14]

His contempt for hurting people sparked a stinging response from Jesus: *You HYPOCRITE!*

A hypocrite is a deceiver. A charlatan in a position of leadership, leads people astray. This religious ruler was so intent on following the letter of their law that he missed the greatest opportunity of his life. He had seen God yet he never recognized Him because of his arrogance. He was blinded by religion.

A hypocrite is a traitor who will promise you one thing but will do another.

A hypocrite is a swindler, a cheater, a pretender.

Jesus was conveying a message in that one word: You pretend to represent God but inside you are a cruel and insensitive person. You who were entrusted with the laws of God have perverted them by adding to them. You have segregated and divided people to suit your own bigoted scheme.

Cultivation Or Indoctrination?

Religion paints a distorted picture of God. This ruler did not recognize God in the flesh because he only knew the God his religion had formed in his mind. He knew a harsh, macho God but did

59

not recognize God in the gentle, loving Jesus.

Religion has been called an opiate that prevents people from detecting its trickery and induces inaction.

Religion is an attitudinizer. Religious teachers, like this ruler of the synagogue where Jesus was teaching, form people's attitudes toward God — and each other, by their biased teachings. Our habitual modes of regarding people (and especially women) come from religion. When we believe on Jesus and accept Him as Lord and Savior of our lives, we can then be delivered from the *spirit* of religion.

When the *spirit* of religion is gone from us, then we can receive the Holy Spirit of God and cultivate the God-given ability to become like Christ.

Guard your attitude by examining the seeds sown in your mind. Check them against the life and teachings of Jesus. Repel the false seeds; receive the seeds of truth.

* * *

Now that we have had a glimpse of the religious ruler, we can turn our attention back to the woman who was at the center of the action at the synagogue on the sabbath.

She stood between:

> religion and right
> loathing and love
> tradition and truth
> contempt and compassion
> disgrace and His grace.

And she came out a winner.

Why was she at the synagogue? She was not allowed in the main worship area which was reserved for male Jews.

Belief Based On Bias

Separation was the principle upon which both temple and synagogue worship were founded. They emphasized the distinction between humanity and God, Jew and Gentile, men and women, priests and people.

The temple building, including the foyer, was divided into six separate areas or courts, rising one above another.

The Court of the Gentiles was the only part to which foreigners were admitted. This court was also located on the lowest level and was outside the actual temple proper.

The Sacred Enclosure was three feet above the Gentile Court. Gentiles were forbidden to pass beyond their allocated area, under penalty of death.

The Court of Women (sometimes called The Treasury) was three feet higher than the Sacred Enclosure, into which Jewish women were permitted to come. However, the women were not allowed to go beyond their court.

The Court of Israel was ten feet higher than the Court of Women and only male Jews could enter.

The Court of Priests was yet three feet above the Court of Israel, which was reserved for priests.

The House of God was eight feet above the Court of the Priests, and was divided into two compartments, The Holy Place and The Holy of Holies. Priests entered into the Holy Place to perform certain duties at stated times, but only the high priest could enter the Holy of Holies once a year, on the Day of Atonement.

The exclusion of the Gentiles from the actual temple proper, showed that the Jews regarded themselves as the chosen people of God and therefore, completely separated themselves from other nations.

The different levels of the courts and the prohibitions concerning access to them, emphasized the strict class distinctions in the Jewish system of religion.

The inaccessibility of the Holy of Holies to all, except the high priest on one day each year, was a continual object lesson concerning the holiness of God and His separation from people.

Imposed Religious Isolation

Jewish synagogues were patterned after their temples.

The form and internal arrangement of the synagogue would depend on the wealth of the Jews who erected it, and where it was built. But there are certain traditional peculiarities which have united Jewish synagogues of all ages and countries.

One such traditional oddity is the segregation of the women from the worship area. They were confined to a separate, usually upper gallery or behind a partition of lattice-work where they could not be seen.

Religious isolation, discriminating barriers and pious restrictions were visible at the synagogue the day the woman bent double met Jesus in person. But why was she there? What motivated her to climb the staircase up to the women's gallery? Was religion her stimulus? Or had she heard that Jesus would be at the synagogue on the sabbath?

Tradition Or Truth?

Religion does interesting things to women. All

over the world I have seen different religions at work. I have decided that the culture of a nation, her traditions, her customs and her attitudes take shape in the mold of her religion. Religion is a strong force, but the power of Jesus is stronger. Religious habit may have gotten the woman to the synagogue on the sabbath, but one greater than religion and greater than the sabbath met her need.

God's love and compassion for womankind was wonderfully demonstrated that day. If culture, tradition and religion are holding you back, or are bending you to a submissive, subservient level, Jesus' declaration is for you: Woman, be free! Woman, you are loosed!

I have seen the twins which religion gives birth to — culture and tradition. Religious women often go through life doing what they are expected to do rather than what they choose to do. They live with obligations rather than options. They bow to rules and requirements instead of enjoying the pleasure of responding to and of cultivating God's ability within them.

As a woman, always remember: Your designated place is following Jesus, and your submission is to Christ. This is God's good news for you. He paid a big price for your FREEDOM. Be free from your shackles.[Jn.8:36]

So Christ has made us free. Now make sure that you

stay free and don't get all tied up again in the chains of slavery to Jewish laws and ceremonies. $^{Ga.5:1\ LB}$

Limited, Labeled But Learning

This woman with physical limitations put forth the effort necessary to get to the synagogue. I believe she had heard that Jesus was there. That is why she was there. Also, I believe that Jesus knew she was coming. He also knows all about you. As you are reading this good news, Jesus is ready to make contact with you. Be sensitive to His voice. Do what He tells you to do just like the woman bent double did, and you too will be totally free today.

As a woman, do not accept the submissive, silent, inferior role that you have been assigned by religion and by culture. When you accept Jesus as Lord of your life, you have no other master. He desires to express His love and leadership through you.

The woman believer (Christian) who accepts cultural restrictions and religious restraints is limiting Jesus who craves expression through her. Only *she* can limit Christ at work in and through her life. *Your body is the temple of the Holy Ghost.* $^{1Co.6:19}$ The Holy Spirit of God in a woman is not meant to be silent. This is good news. Believe it and live in complete freedom.

No rabbi had ever done what Jesus did that day

in the synagogue. But Jesus was more than a rabbi. He was God in the flesh. I can just see Him as He was teaching, looking all around. He saw the ruler of the synagogue, then some important Jewish men in their special seats of honor, then the sanctuary full of patriarchal Jews. But Jesus kept looking, penetrating the barrier which concealed and shut off the women. I see His full attention centering on that limited, labeled woman of low esteem.

Hallmarking Womankind

As He looked beyond and above those proper, pious, prejudiced men, anticipation, hope and faith were born in the women's gallery. Every eye was on Jesus! God was going into action! It was time for a denouncement of divisions, a proclamation of priorities, the hallmarking of womankind and the silencing of the self-righteous.

Jesus called the woman forward to where He was.[Lu.13:12] In that invitation, the woman heard love and compassion. That gave her the strength and courage to obey His call. She trusted Jesus more than she feared the religious system.

It takes courage to be what God created her to be. She can be a Jesus-woman if she does not fear what people say about her; if she accepts God's will and lets go of the sanctimonious patriarchal indoctrination she may have inherited.

Jesus called the woman to himself in the presence of everyone. He was not ashamed to identify with her and her need. He is not ashamed of you. He identifies with you as you are, where you are. Be courageous and trust Him. His attitude toward this woman shows God's character, His nature.

Jesus has not changed, but He changed:

sabbath to sanction
restriction to restoration
isolation to realization
ruling to reigning
degradation to jubilation
resignation to decision
bondage to freedom
chains to change

And Jesus Christ is the same yesterday, and today, and forever.[He.13:8]

Courageous And Cured

When I read about this woman who was bent double, I always think of women around the world. I have seen so many of them in this same physical, mental and spiritual condition.

The mother of Kariuki, the madman who was delivered from demons in one of our East African crusades, was just such a woman. From early childhood she had carried loads far beyond her physical capacity. As a result, she was bent double and could not lift herself up.

After her son was miraculously restored to sanity, Kariuki's mother decided to put forth the effort to come to our gospel crusade. This was not easy because she was bent double, the area was hilly and the multitude was vast. Her struggle paid off. For the first time in her life she heard the good news of Jesus. Then she accepted Him as her personal savior. She was instantly freed from her bondage. She could stand up, bend, jump, run and was completely healed. She was a totally freed woman.

Jesus is still calling women who are bent under impossible burdens to come to where He is. He cares about you. He desires to lift your burdens and to give you strength to stand up, free from your psychological, physical and spiritual bondage. He wants to minister to the needs of hurting people through you.

Identified, Dignified And Justified

In order for this woman to go to the part of the synagogue where Jesus was, it required a great deal of faith, trust and courage on her part. She left the segregated gallery, ascended the stairs cautiously and transcended the *sacred* threshold of the men's area. Every head was turned in her direction. Every eye was fixed either on Jesus, or the woman, the object of His love.

There is a price that must be paid for freedom, and she was paying the price. She risked being killed by religious purists. Jesus was also at risk because Jewish Law prescribed a stiff penalty for defiling the sabbath or for doing any *work* on that day.^{Ex.31:14; Nu.15:32-35} The religious rulers considered healing to be *work*.

As the woman bent double held on to her ankles for support, she inched her way toward the speaker. You see, Jesus could have met her at the doorway to save her any humiliation or reprisal. Somehow, I believe it was necessary for her to totally penetrate the worship area and to reach Jesus at that very sacred spot in the synagogue. What a message of liberation was being demonstrated.

As she entered the main area of worship, Jesus spoke to her and said, *Woman, you are loosed from your infirmity.*^{Lu.13:12} *Then as she came near, Jesus laid His hands on her.*^{Lu.13:13} Why did Jesus proceed to lay His hands on this woman? He had spoken and His words had brought healing. Was that not sufficient?

Greater Than The Law

It is wonderful to see the very nature of our heavenly Father being shown in His only begotten Son, Jesus. Religious tradition and culture had already depreciated women to a lower status than men, had sentenced them to servitude and shame in the name of God and had even excluded them from direct access to Him.

In this one encounter Jesus had already violated four Jewish laws. He had:

1 - Spoken to the woman in public;

2 - Brought her into the area reserved for men — the alleged superior sex;

3 - Brought her to the speaker's platform, a very holy place in the synagogue;

4 - Healed her, which was *work* on the sabbath.

Now He would commit a 5th violation: He touched this woman in public. Here were five violations of religious law that became five steps of grace, mercy and truth.

The woman cooperated. She was obedient. She was courageous. She cast religious rules and regulations aside and accepted Jesus as being greater than tradition and culture. In order to be freed from her shackles it was necessary for her to go all the way and to do everything that Jesus asked her to do. Because she was obedient to Him, she was made whole.

Change Your World

As a woman, you are no different. Go all out for

Jesus in spite of any tradition that curtails you and be made completely whole psychologically, physically and spiritually. Release your religious hang-ups. They will never lead you to God.

Woman, BE FREE! What a command! What a declaration! What an opportunity! When Jesus says you can, you must. Woman, be free!

You are set at liberty from the dominion of Satan. Sin no longer has power over you. You no longer need to submit to the control of another person. *Woman, Be Free,* in the name of Jesus. Decide to be free now!

You are unchained from religious restrictions. You are free from your psychological problems. Woman, be free! You are valuable. Jesus esteems you. You are important to God's dream for humankind. He needs you to minister love to people. God wills to show His magnificent mercy through you. Do not keep silent. Speak up for your Liberator, Jesus Christ.

Be as courageous in your approach to Jesus as that disabled woman was in Bible days. For eighteen years she had been unable to stand upright. How demoralizing that must have been. How many sabbaths had come and gone? How many trips had she made to the synagogue? The day Jesus met her there, her world was changed. Jesus will change you too. Then you can change your world.

Woman, you are loosed from your infirmity.[Lu.13:12]
You are released. You are forgiven. You are pardoned. You are liberated.

Jesus made that pronouncement for time and eternity. He made it for you. *Woman, BE FREE!* Woman, you are loosed! You can preach. You can teach. You can be a Jesus-woman! Be free from the top of your head to the bottom of your feet. Be courageous and cooperate with Jesus. He is calling you to Him. He is telling you: *Woman, you are loosed from your infirmity.* Accept His liberation and be made whole.

Jesus said, *Woman, you are loosed.* Your bond is broken. Your chains are dissolved. You are unrestrained.

Prioritizing Humankind

You may be like that woman. She had been looking at feet while others were seeing a beautiful blue sky. She saw impossibilities while others saw opportunities. She was restricted and limited while others were unlimited and had no controls. Jesus gave her power to stand up, to step up, to look up and to rise up to a status she had never known before. All things became possible because she had courage and confidence.

Woman, BE FREE! Jesus sets you free. *When the Son makes you free, you are indeed free.*[Jn.8:36] *You shall know the truth and the truth shall set you free.*[Jn.18:32]

72

Jesus confronted the religious system. He brought a new day to womankind. He introduced a new world of thought. He ushered in new possibilities and opportunities. And He took His message to the center of religion, to the platform of orthodox authority.

He reflected God's attitude toward female human persons. No other teacher had stood in the synagogue and resolutely overruled five religious laws in order to prioritize a woman. What Jesus did then, He did for you as well as for that disabled woman. He showed how unorthodox God is, how available He is and how no ordinance of religion can change, control or opinionate God. God is Love! He has always been and will always be, Love. If your religion teaches otherwise, Jesus says to you, *Woman, you are free!* Walk out of your bondage. Walk toward Jesus just like that woman did. When she reached Him, she was made whole.

Tradition Can Terrorize

If you have been terrorized or censored by religious rulers; if tradition has you bent and bound; turn to Jesus. When you make contact with Him, your shackles will dissolve whether they are religious, psychological, physical or spiritual. *Be free,* in the name of Jesus.

Jesus sets you free from negative thoughts,

from guilt, from self-condemnation, from feelings of inferiority, timidity, fear, anxiety and depression.

Jesus sets women free from alcoholism and from drugs. When you are made whole by Jesus, your desires, thoughts and habits change. Religion cannot change you. Jesus can and does because He gives you a new life, His life.

A young prostitute came to one of our meetings. She sold her body to support her drug habit. She had been in and out of prison but that never changed her. A leopard cannot change its spots. But when she heard the gospel, she discovered new purpose for her life. She accepted Jesus as her personal savior. Her life was completely transformed and she set out on a mission of love to lead depraved human beings to Jesus.

What a transformation takes place when a life is touched by Jesus. He forgives, heals and restores in just a moment of time. Religion cannot do this for you, but Jesus can and will. Woman, you are loosed from your shackles. BE FREE, in Jesus' name.

Beautiful, Positive, Wonderful

In the synagogue on that sabbath day, the religious ruler became very angry. An authority higher than his had spoken. Jesus, the Son of God, did not submit to rules. He just did something beautiful and positive and wonderful for one of God's creation. That act of love drew the hypocrite out of his corner. Then the people could see the difference between religion and love at work. They could make a choice. They could choose Jesus or religion. They could follow religion which saw only the importance of a rule being violated, or they could accept Jesus who saw a broken human person and took the initiative to make her whole.

Basically, those are the same options we have today — religion or Jesus. They are not synonymous. They represent different worlds. They lead to different destinies. One is death, the other is life. Jesus said: *I am the way, the truth, and the life. Whoever has God's Son has life; whoever does not have His Son, does not have life.*^{Jn.14:6}

Jesus challenged the haughty *hypocrite: Does not each of you on the sabbath loose your ox or ass from the stall and lead it away to water?* ^{Lu.13:15}

And ought not this woman, whom Satan has bound for eighteen years be loosed from this bondage on the sabbath day? ^{Lu.13:16}

This *hypocrite* was outwardly concerned about religion, but inwardly, he was a cruel, insensitive person. He had more concern for an animal than he did for a human person created in God's image. He would gladly unshackle an ox so it could satisfy its thirst on the sabbath. Yet he was angered when Jesus unshackled that woman on the sabbath.

This disabled woman had a thirst that only Jesus could quench. He dissolved her shackles and she drank until she was satisfied.

Eclipsing Religion

Jesus introduced a set of values which eclipsed those of religion.

Jesus released womankind from the bondage and harshness of religious rules and introduced the human race to mercy and forgiveness. Therefore, you need not stay bent down under ordinances and coercions.

Woman, be free! You are special. You are a unique creation of your heavenly Father. He sent His Son, Jesus, to show you how much He cares for you. He needs you. He believes in you. You are important to His dream for humankind.

Jesus is your Liberator, your Friend, your Savior. Jesus is your Healer, your Provider, your Peace, your Protection. Jesus gives you pardon, peace, pride, and purpose.

The attitude of other people cannot hurt you. Your attitude is what counts. What is your attitude? Do you choose to follow Jesus? Are you free? Are your shackles gone?

After the woman in bondage was set free, what do you think she did? Did her life remain as it was before? I think not. I believe she became one of those who followed Jesus as He went from town to town showing the multitudes how much God loved them.

You are ready to take that step right now. Accept Jesus as your personal savior. Take these five easy but vital steps. You can do it now.

The first step is: Recognize that *all have sinned and all fall short of God's glorious ideal.*[Ro.3:23] Sin separates you from God.

The second step is: Repent, be sorry for your sins. *Except you repent you will perish.*[Lu.13:3] *And remember, God so loved the world, that He gave His only begotten Son, that whoever believes in Him should not perish, but have everlasting life.*[Jn.3:16]

The third step is: Confess your sins to God. *He/she that covers sin shall not prosper; but whoever confesses and forsakes their sins shall have mercy.*[Pr.28:13]

If we confess our sins, God is faithful and just to forgive our sins and to cleanse us from all unrighteousness.[1Jn.1:9]

The fourth step is: Ask God to forgive you for every sin you have ever committed. *In Jesus Christ we have redemption through His blood, the forgiveness of sins according to the riches of His grace.*[Ep.1:7]

And the fifth step is: Receive Jesus as Savior. *For if you tell others with your own mouth that Jesus Christ is your Lord, and believe in your own heart that God has raised Him from the dead, you will be saved.* Ro.10:9-10

You can make contact with Jesus right now.

Pray this prayer with me. And remember: Praying is simply talking to God who is your loving heavenly Father. He receives you with love.

Dear heavenly Father, thank You for sending Your Son, Jesus, to be my Liberator.

Thank You for loving me so much that You provided a way out of my bondage of sin.

You gave Your Son, Jesus, who gave His life for me.

That demonstrates the value You place on me as a woman.

Father, I accept Your forgiveness and Your life through Jesus Christ.

Thank You, Jesus, for showing me that I do have a choice.

I choose to be a follower of Jesus Christ -- a Jesus-person; and I choose to never limit you in my life because I am a woman.

Thank You, Father, for the gift of FREEDOM. I accept it in Jesus' name.

From this day, You are my loving Lord and gentle Master.

Thank You, Father, that I am now a part of Your FREEDOM-dream for all human persons. I am one of your royal daughters in Your divine family.

My life now has meaning and purpose.

Thank You, Jesus.

Amen.

Now, you too have heard the liberating words of Jesus: *Woman ... be free!* You can rise up and stand up with pride, loosed from the bondage of religious tradition and culture. You are freed from inferiority, timidity and feelings of worthlessness.

You are valuable. You are a Jesus-person. Your life now has new and exciting dimensions of hope and happiness, of forgiveness and fulfillment, of peace and purpose ... from this very day!

God bless you!

WOMEN & SELF-ESTEEM

III

LIVING
IS
CHOOSING

WHY DO SOME women act? And others react? Why do some depend upon the opinions of friends? While others trust their own?

In every experience, a woman has the choice of becoming bitter or better; fearful or loving; haughty or humble; hateful or grateful.

Every woman has obstacles to overcome that are the result of roles established by culture.

The good news for you is that God has a beautiful plan for your life. Choose Jesus Christ and let Him direct you according to His design.

Your faith in God is expressed by your faith in people.

Your love for God is expressed by your love for people.

When Jesus is at the center of your world, your words — your influence — create a beautiful and a terrific world.

Look at what you have. Look at what you know. Look at what you can do. Remember that God never slots women in limiting roles.

Chapter 3

LIVING IS CHOOSING

IN THIS CHAPTER, you as a woman will discover how simple it is to become all that God has in mind for you to be. His plan for you is beautiful.

The following phrases reflect my life goal and portray the way that I have lived my life. They were penned by Amanda Bradley, a woman poet.

Lord, let me be a dreamer and let me be a doer. Let me strive and steadily achieve.

Let me be a learner and let me be a teacher. Let me give and graciously receive.

Let me be Your follower. Let me be Your friend. Let me hear Your voice and heed Your call.

Let me come to know the special plans You have for me. And let me with Your help, fulfill them all.

In order to realize total fulfillment in life, you must learn the importance of choosing.

Have you ever wondered why some women are negative? And why others are positive? Why some systematically fail? And others consistently succeed?

Why do some women act? And others react? Why do some depend upon the opinions of friends? While others trust their own?

Why are some women always demeaned or humiliated? And others are always complimented or honored?

You Are Included

The book of Romans was written by Paul, for women the same as for men. He was born a Jew, a practiced Pharisee, but he was converted and he became a Christian, a born-again follower of Jesus. This letter was written to non-Jews, to Gentiles (that includes each of us), and hand-carried from Corinth to Rome, by Paul's right hand woman, Phoebe.

Dear friends in Rome. This letter is from Paul, Christ's slave, chosen to be a missionary, and sent out to preach God's Good News about His Son, Jesus Christ our Lord, who came as a human baby. And being raised from the dead, He was proven to be the mighty Son of God with the holy nature of God Himself. (Just like you and me. And now through Christ, all the kindness of God has been poured out upon us sinners, and now He is sending us out around the world to tell all people everywhere the great things God has done for them so that they too will believe and obey Him.

And you, dear friends, are among those He dearly loves. You too are invited by Jesus Christ to be God's very own, yes, His holy people.[Ro.1:1-7 LB]

So now, since we have been made right in God's sight by faith in His promises and because of our faith, Christ has brought us into this place of highest privilege where we now stand.

We, as believers, do not back up nor move over; we stand upon our redemptive rights and we move forward. *And we look with confidence and joy.* Why? *Because we can actually, become all that God had in His mind for us to be.*[Ro.5:2 LB]

Revealing Reflection

T.L. and I were on the USS Marine Panther enroute to India in 1945. I was reading Aimee Semple McPherson's story. As a young woman, she and her husband had gone to India as missionaries.

During their ministry there, Aimee's husband and her little boy became very ill. It was not long before she buried her husband in China's soil. Aimee came home as a nineteen-year-old widow with her little son.

Reflecting back on that experience, it amazes

me that these sad facts were what impressed me about Aimee Semple McPherson's life and ministry. There were many positive and successful experiences which I could have remembered. She witnessed many miracles. The influence of her life was outstanding.

But none of those events impressed me at the time. The death and burial of her husband, her becoming a widow, her coming home broken hearted with her baby, were the events I remembered.

Why? Perhaps it was because I was a young mother, a young wife on my way to India with my husband. And Aimee's experience was relating to me in a negative way because I received only the negative message of the story. That need not have been the case.

The Voice Of Choice

Do you know why some women are negative? Why others are positive? Or why the same woman is sometimes positive and sometimes negative?

It has to do with the choices we make. We are constantly making them, you know. Every time we see something, or hear something, or read something, we instantly make a choice. We like it, or we do not like it. We believe it, or we do not believe it. We accept it, or we reject it. The way we respond is determined by our own choice in each situation.

We either choose the opportunity in a situation or we overlook it.

Right now, you are choosing how this book is going to affect your life. In every experience, a woman has the choice of becoming bitter or better; fearful or fateful; haughty or humble; hateful or grateful.

You are the one who makes the choice.

When I was young, the term *used of God* was quite popular. But I have learned since, that God does not *use* women. He gives to women the stuff to *use*. He gives to us the ability to choose. And He respects our right of choice. There has been enough *use* and *abuse* and *mis-use* of women's choice-power.

The good news for you is that God has a beautiful plan for your life. He has a design, a plan, a program for your life. All you have to do is to choose to link yourself with Jesus Christ and to let Him direct you according to His design.

Always look for the opportunity in each situation that you face as a woman. Exercise your ability to choose. Decide to be on God's side. The more you follow Christ in every detail of your life, the more confidence you will have. You will discover that it is not difficult to know God's will for your life. That is how you learn to become all that God wants you as a woman, to be.

Your Hidden Power

Sometimes, women argue that it is easier to move with the crowd. It is more comfortable to be like other women. There is more security in doing what everyone else is doing. But remember, when Jesus looks at you, He does not see the crowd or the mass. He sees you individually.

This is the principle which T.L., my husband, and I practice in ministering to the multitudes who throng our crusades abroad. We pioneered the modern concept of mass evangelism all over the world. But we do not see the people as a *mass;* we see them as *individuals.*

People often ask us, *How many were in the multitude today?* And we usually answer, *We don't know.* When you cannot see the end of the crowd, when you cannot see the sides of the crowd, how many people are there? To us, it's just a field of individuals with tremendous needs and a ravishing hunger for the good news of Jesus Christ.

When ministering to those enormous masses of people, we have great confidence because we know that God is seeing each individual, and that He is concerned with each person.

That is how He is looking at *you* right now.

No matter what other women or men may do, you are free to make an individual choice to be different, unique and to become all that God wants you to be.

It is not usually easy to be the unique woman or man which God created you to be. It requires effort and discipline. It requires that you continually make positive choices that involve Him in your life. By choosing, you use the power that God has given you to make things happen.

You are your own miracle, in that sense. That is not *humanism,* — not when you believe in God, and in Jesus Christ, and when you do what God wants you to do through His power, and according to His word.

Confines Of Culture

Culture does not make it easy for a woman, to be all that God wants her to be.

What is culture? I sometimes say that *religion* had twins. One was called *culture,* the other was called *tradition.*

Every woman (and each man) has obstacles to overcome that are the result of roles established by culture. T.L. and I have observed how little girls and boys are cast into these roles from the time they are born?

God does not slot people into limiting roles. I

89

am Daisy Washburn Osborn. I am blessed because I am married to T.L. Osborn. We are sweethearts, we are friends, we are companions and spouses. Being a wife, a mother, a grandmother and a great-grandmother does not change the fact of *who* I am. I am still Daisy Washburn Osborn, the unique individual that God created. The role that society places on me does not dictate God's plan for me.

Culture and tradition — the twins of religion — usually try to keep women from becoming what God wants them to be.

But if you have enough faith, enough love, enough courage, enough trust in God and love for God, you will make it.

Your faith in God is expressed by your faith in people.

Your love for God is expressed by your love for people.

If you care about your world and if you practice using your God-given choice power, then you can surmount anything. You can accomplish anything. And you can do it with dignity and grace.

Freedom Demonstrated

Maria Woodworth-Etter (1844-1924) was a woman ahead of her time.

She was saved when she was 12 years old. Maria heard the voice of Jesus saying, *Go out and gather lost sheep.* But in the late 1800's the church did not allow women to preach the gospel. That tradition delayed her obedience to God for a long time. Finally, Maria told the Lord, *When I grow up, I'll marry a missionary; then I'll serve You.*

But that was not what God had in mind. His plan for Maria's life was not limited by the religious standards of her day. God never gives up on His dream for people. And finally Maria said, *Yes.*

That remarkable woman preached the gospel until she was 80 years old. She had a tremendous ministry in the face of all kinds of odds. And remember, this was in the late 1800's and the early 1900's ... before the current political emphasis on the constitutional rights of women. People were tough and had no tolerance for a woman preacher. But she succeeded in becoming all that God wanted her to be. She preached to hundreds of thousands of people, face to face, all across the nation. And her preaching was confirmed by hundreds of the most extra-ordinary healing miracles and remarkable conversions ever recorded in the history of evangelism in America.

The last words that Maria Woodworth-Etter said were, *What God did in the past, He will do in the future.* What a prophecy-testimony. And this is the profound truth which we have witnessed during our more than five decades of ministry to millions around the world.

What God did in the past, He does now, and He will do in the future. This is a new generation. And you are part of it. God shows Himself again and again — to each generation. Paul said, *He never left Himself without a witness.*^Ac.14:17 LB He never changes. He reveals Himself afresh to each new generation and keeps doing the same things. He keeps loving people, in spite of all of the negative traditions and limiting cultures which humankind contrives.

Women, it was Maria Woodworth-Etter's day then, and she chose to obey God. This is your day. Here are five important questions which concern the vital choices you will be called upon to make in life.

No. 1.

Why Choose To Be All That God Wants You To Be?

The No. 1 priority of the church — of each believer — is to evangelize the world. Is this your priority as a woman?

Ask these questions, and decide for yourself as a woman, if reaching people is important to you?

What do you do with your money? What do you do with your time? What do you do with your talents? Are you doing anything to reach out to win souls for Christ?

If your answers reveal that you are not engaged in God's No. 1 priority, you can choose to re-begin and to decide to be all that God wants you to be.

No. 2.

Who Should Choose To Be Involved In God's Plan?

Believers. Women, men, girls and boys. The No. 1 opportunity of every believer is to share Christ. That is evangelism. That is a No. 1 choice for life.

You do not need to ask God to send you to China. Begin right where you are. Give the gospel to your family, to those in your neighborhood, to your community, your town, your state, and your nation. Just keep reaching out. You will discover that once you begin, doors will keep opening to you. Your gender will not hinder you unless you allow it to.

The compelling fact is: When you know Christ, your priority as a woman, is to share Christ.

When you receive life, your priority is to share life with others.

When you are healed, your priority is to be a healing influence for others.

When you are blessed, your priority is to be a blessing to someone else.

When you accept God's forgiveness, your priority is to practice forgiveness toward others.

When you receive love, your priority is to express love to those who need love.

That is the lifestyle of a believer. Does that sound too simple? It is simple. The key is awareness. Practice being aware of the Jesus who is living in you, making you into all that God planned for you as a woman, to be.

Be aware by saying to yourself, *Jesus is in me. I am seeing this individual through the eyes of Jesus who has no eyes on this earth but my eyes. He is looking through me.*

Yes, God's arms reach around the world. But those arms are the arms of human persons — of believers like you. It was God's choice to use human beings to reach human beings with the gospel, and He never limited our reach by our race, our status, or our gender.

He chose you and me to do His work. Personally, I choose to do Christ's work. How about you?

No. 3.

Where Can You Choose To Demonstrate God's Plan?

In your world. Your world needs your influence. What is your world? It is the world that surrounds you.

Your influence has tremendous creative power in your world. Here is why: Each of us has the power to create around us the kind of world we want. That power is seed-power. And our seeds are our words, our thoughts, our actions. With these, we influence the people in our world. That is how we grow people around us to be what God wants them to be.

When Jesus is at the center of your world, your words — your influence — create a beautiful and a terrific world around you.

Choose to be all that God wants you to be. Forget your race or your sex. Decide — choose to obey your Lord.

And this gospel of the Kingdom shall be preached in all the world for a witness to all nations, then shall the end come.^{Mt.24:14}

Remember that we are not to just go to the nations that will give us a visa. If the early Christians had only preached and witnessed where it was legal, the gospel may not have spread throughout their world as it did. The Bible says, *there was great persecution against the church ... therefore they (men and WOMEN) that were scattered abroad went everywhere preaching the word.*[Ac.8:1-4]

From Prison To Divine Commission

A gang of drug smugglers came to Jesus Christ in one of our meetings in California. They had been in prison for smuggling cocaine across the Mexican border into Southern California. They had a billion dollar drug business.

Then they were wonderfully converted, all of them. A wife, a husband, their children, his brother, their father and mother, father-in-law and mother-in-law, uncles, aunts, cousins — the whole family accepted Jesus Christ. They were radiant with the light of the gospel.

I said to them, *Do not lose your ability to smuggle. Right now, about ninety percent of the world can only receive the gospel as it is smuggled to them by believers.*

That family of *smugglers* was so relieved to hear me tell them that God had a plan for them, and that they did not have to change their trade or to bury their talent. All they had to do was to utilize their talent smuggling the right substance — *the gospel.*

That is the way that God accepts people. That is the way He accepts you. He takes you where you are and makes your life into something beautiful for people — for His Kingdom.

Sow It And Grow It

This Gospel must be published among all nations.^{Mk.13:10} That is why we print literature by the tons and distribute it around the world, in 132 different languages.

And I beheld a great multitude which no one could number, of all nations, tribes, peoples and tongues, standing before the throne, and before the Lamb, clothed in white robes, with palm branches in their hands, and crying out with a loud voice saying, Salvation belongs to our God who sits on the throne, and to the Lamb.^{Re.7:9-10}

Are you going to choose to become all that God wants you to be? Everywhere He wants you to be? Women and men — every believer, every follower of Christ, you and I are the ones.

Do you sometimes feel that you are not yet ready to launch out and to do the things which God has in mind for you? My counsel to you is — *begin.* You are ready for the first step now, and you will become ready for tomorrow's challenges by the steps that you take today.

You will learn by teaching.

You will gain by giving.

You will reap by sowing.

You will grow by sharing.

This is God's formula for your success.

Do you want to go some place? Do you want to achieve a goal? Do you want to accomplish something? I have just given you the formula.

We grow with God as we grow with people.

We live with God, as we live with people.

It is wonderful to be involved with people.

Permission Granted

I encourage you as a woman, to choose to be all that God wants you to be.

Why? Only women can change the world of women, and there are many more women than men in the world today. Some estimate that three-fourths of all committed believers are women.

Joel prophesied, *And it shall come to pass afterward, that I will pour out my Spirit upon all flesh; and your sons and your daughters shall prophesy.*[Jl.2:28]

Women, only you can change your world. Choose to do just that. You do not need anyone's permission. You have been given your orders by the highest authority — your Lord.

You have been commissioned by Jesus. Do not wait for a council of elders, a board of theologians, an order of priests, or a cardinal to tell you what you can do.

You have your orders. You know what you are authorized to do. Just go and do it. Go and share Christ with your hurting world.

Welcome Change

The woman who sees her identity in Jesus Christ is a peacemaker. She is humble. She is willing to serve anyone, anytime, anywhere. And those who have their identity in Jesus Christ will surface to the top every time. That kind of service is the greatest kind of leadership.

Look at what you have. Look at what you know. Look at what you can do. Do not be concerned about what you do not know, or what you do not have, or what you cannot do.

Do what you can do. Give what you have. Be what you are. Share what you know. And watch yourself grow.

People will say, *What in the world has happened to you? You used to be so shy. You used to be so quiet.*

The answer is simple. You discovered your choice power and you began to really *live*.

Jesus said in essence: *Do you want to be the great-*

est in the Kingdom of God. Become a believer, a follower, a disciple and then graduate with the degree, Servant of All. Mk.10:43-44

Women and men, there are no limits. You can choose the greatest opportunities that exist in the ministry of Christ — helping people.

No. 4.

When Do We Choose?

Today. There have never been as many people living on the earth as there are today. There have never been as many needs to fill or as many problems to solve as there are today. There have never been as many lost people to reach as there are today.

Yet we have never had so many great inventions or so much sophisticated equipment at our disposal as we have today. There are so many facilities that we can use. There is so much knowledge at our disposal. There are so many open doors and so much encouragement. Now is the time to take advantage of the great opportunities which we face today in our hurting world.

The harvest is great. The possibilities have no limits.

The laborers are few. God needs you. You are unique. You are important. No one else can do the job that He has for you.

The time is short. There has never been a better time than now.

Choose to begin today.

Why? Because you are a follower of Jesus Christ.

Who should do it? You. Because you are a believer.

Where should you begin? In your world of influence.

When do you start? Now. Because your world needs you.

No. 5.

HOW Do We Choose?

The first step is to get right with God. Discover God in yourself. You see, you can choose to be all that God wants you to be, everywhere He wants you to be, when you are right with Him.

When you have made the choice to be on His side, involved with Him, that opens the door for you to be all that He wants you to be.

As one of God's partners, I encourage you to embrace this marvelous message of God's great kindness. For God says, *Your cry came to me at a favorable time, when the doors of welcome were wide open.* 2Co.6:1-2 LB

Right now is the time for you to begin to be all that God wants you to be in every dimension of your life.

What are you doing personally to share the gospel? Not, what is your church doing, but what are *you* doing as an individual believer to increase the Kingdom of God? Do you want to become a demonstration of Jesus?

The first step is to get right with God.

Today you can choose to accept the life that God offers to you. He loves you and He desires only good for you. Believe on the Lord Jesus Christ and be born again as you pray this prayer right now:

Thank You, Lord Jesus, for what You did on the cross for me.

You bore my sin.

You bore my sickness.

You gave me your righteousness.

You gave me Your health.

I repent of my sins.

Forgive every wrong I have ever done.

I receive your love and your forgiveness.

I welcome You into my life, Jesus, as my Lord and Savior.

I accept Your health.

Now that You live in me, my body is holy and I know that You want it to be healthy.

I want to be Your ambassador to my world.

See with my eyes.

Hear with my ears.

Speak with my lips.

Smile with my face.

Think with my mind.

Make me into all that You want me to be.

From this day, I will go forward with faith and love and confidence.

I choose to opt for every opportunity to be all that you want me to be.

Thank You, Jesus, for my new life.

Amen.

* * *

Now you are ready to begin. Remember, you are important to God. He is with you and He is in you, to give you the courage that you need for every opportunity, every day of your life.

Today is the day to exercise your wonderful power of choice. It's never too late. Just begin, in Jesus' name.

God bless you!

IV

LEADING
BY
SERVING

JESUS INTRODUCED LEADERSHIP as serving, and servant-hood as the mark of greatness. Jesus was meek; He was gentle; He was a servant. But He was and is the greatest of all leaders.

A true servant is what you become as a woman follower of Christ, through the process of your own choices. You choose to serve. You take the initiative. You are not filling a social role that has been prescribed by society for the female gender. You have embraced the Jesus lifestyle.

Make positive choices. The more choices you make the better choices you can make. Practice decision-making. If you do not make the decisions that concern your life, somebody else will make them for you. Someone else will determine your future. Never surrender this right to another person.

Here is a principle which you as a woman, will want to remember: The risks you take when you make personal choices are not risks at all compared to the vulnerability you expose yourself to by not exercising your right of choice.

Never abandon your own dreams. Your own ambitions in life, your personal goals are important. Commit yourself to seeing them realized. Never give up!

Whatever you do, do it with a servant's mind and heart. You will be astonished at the change this will bring to your life as a woman follower of Christ.

Chapter 4

LEADING BY SERVING

*N*EITHER YOU NOR *anyone else can serve two masters. You will hate one and show loyalty to the other, or you will be enthusiastic about one and despise the other.*Lu.16:13 LB

*The more lowly your service to others, the greater you are. To be the greatest, be a servant. But those who think themselves great shall be disappointed and humbled; and those who humble themselves shall be exalted.*Mt.23:11-12 LB

ANYONE — a woman or a man, *wanting to be greatest must be the least* — *the servant of all!* Mk.9:35 LB

Jesus introduced leadership as serving, and servant-hood as the mark of greatness. He gave us the key to true humility and the formula for genuine meekness. Jesus was meek; He was gentle; He was a servant. But He was and is the greatest of all leaders. We can risk following His teaching and His example. In doing so, He gives us the quality of mind necessary to becoming a servant as He is. That is truly *Leading By Serving,* and it places you in the category of *Women And Self-Esteem.*

When Jesus used the word *servant,* He was not referring to a social class. He was intimating a lifestyle. A servant is not what someone else makes you. If you serve because you are forced to, or because you feel it is your responsibility, you are not a servant. You are a slave.

Choice Is Initiative

Because a woman's *choice*-power is so vital to her success, I am dedicating a second chapter of this book to help women believers practice being aware of their options in life, and to develop the essential skill of exercising their right of choice.

A true servant is what you become as a woman follower of Christ, through the process of your own choices. You choose to serve. You take the initiative. You are not filling a social role that has been prescribed by society for the female gender. You have embraced the Jesus lifestyle.

Jesus said: *In this world the kings and so-called great people order their slaves around. And the slaves have no choice but to like it. But among you believers — followers of Jesus, the one who serves you best — who has chosen to do so — will be your leader.* Lu.22:25-26 LB

108

There is a *slave* mentality or attitude that women can assume through the double-influence of culture and of religion.

There is also a *servant* mentality or attitude that a woman can adopt through understanding the gospel and by embracing the principles shared in Christ's teachings and by His example.

The woman with a *slave* complex, functions on the premise of fear. Whereas the woman with a *servant* deportment functions on the premise of love.

Fear and love are both great motivators. The contrast between the two is seen in the result of deeds done out of fear as opposed to those done out of love. The effect on the performer of deeds done out of fear is: resentment, bitterness, revenge, restraint, pessimism, oppression and unhappiness — just to name a few.

However, the effect on the performer of deeds done out of love is: acceptance, harmony, forgiveness, freedom, optimism, courage, happiness and total fulfillment.

A slave is a person whose personal life is controlled by the moods, the attitudes, the demands, the priorities and the desires of another person.

A slave is a person whose own goals, desires, talents, abilities and ambitions suffer fetal paralysis because they have surrendered their right of choice to another person.

Freedom From Domination

If there is a person in your life who constantly forces you to modify your desires, shift your priorities, shirk your chosen responsibilities, surrender your dreams and neglect your needs, then there is an area of your life where you are a slave, and you are submitting to a self-appointed master. When you surrender to a human master, you do so out of fear. When you surrender to Jesus, you do so out of love.

The gospel of Jesus Christ does not make slaves of women. The gospel sets a woman free from all bondage. Believe and receive Jesus as your Savior and Lord. Then you will be truly free from all forms of slavery. You can then choose greatness and become a real leader.

The gospel is the good news that you as a woman, are free from chains. When you are truly free from bondage, you do not bow to the domination of others; nor do you attempt to control other people.

Jesus said: *You are truly My disciple if you live as I tell you to, and you will know the truth and the truth will set you free.**Jn.8:31-32 LB* The freedom that Jesus offers is freedom from the dominion of sin and freedom from the possessiveness and the domination of other people. Know Jesus. Know the truth that the gospel presents.

As a woman, you have a choice. First of all, choose Jesus. When you do this, you are freed from your old master, Satan and all of his submasters.

The greatest servant who ever lived was Jesus. He chose to be a servant. He is our example, our leader, our Lord, our Master.

Commitment To Freedom

The gospel of Jesus Christ even frees a woman from religion.

Religion offers its own invented doctrines, superstitions and corrupted opinions in order to enslave the minds and lives of women in particular.

Paul said regarding the religious men who tried to combine Jewish laws with the teachings of Jesus: *They tried to get us all tied up in their rules, like slaves in chains.*[Ga.2:4 LB]

Paul said: *Thank God that though you once chose to be slaves of sin, now you have obeyed with all your heart the teaching to which God has committed you* (and you have committed your life to Him as a result). *Now you are free from your old master, sin* (and Satan); *And now you have become servants to your new master which is righteousness,* (which is Jesus, which is God).[Ro.6:16-18 LB]

That happens through your choices, your decisions. You have the right of choice. You can act decisively.

When your right to choose is taken from you, you are reduced to the level of a slave. This can happen little by little. It pays to practice making decisions, for when you do, you are exercising your choice-ability. Like any other skill, it improves with unwearied use.

The Art Of Choosing

As a woman, if you do not make the decisions that concern your life, someone else will make those decisions for you. Someone else will determine your future. Never surrender this right to another person.

Your choices are what determine how you live, how you prosper, how you are blessed and how productive your life is as a woman. You cannot blame someone else for your problems, for your failures, for your misery, for your predicament. Make a choice. Choose to change your situation.

When Jesus directs your life, when you are His follower, He will give you ideas that will inspire solutions to the problems you may confront. Those divine ideas will turn your failures into favors and successes, your misery into mirth and your desperate situations into positive, productive opportunities.

Here is a principle which you as a woman, will want to remember: The risks you take when you make personal choices are not risks at all compared to the vulnerability you expose yourself to by not exercising your right of choice.

God created every woman with a will. We are constantly exercising that will. God never violates our will or our choices but He guides us in His way of success as we allow His word to keep us tuned to His wave-lengths. We may even make a bad choice, but He never gives up on us, because He has given us the power to make another choice to correct the bad one.

When you choose Jesus, then you are free from Satan's power and he is no longer your master, then you are no longer his slave. Jesus becomes your Lord, your Leader and your Master. You become His servant; you become His physical expression on this earth.

You can serve only one master and the choice of masters is the right of every woman to make.

Symptoms Of Slavery

When you hear the word, *slave*, do you automatically think of history and the slaves in chains? Every nation has had them in some epoch of their history, and they still exist in many societies, though they are not any more called by the old-fashioned, demeaning term, *slaves*.

Slaves come in all colors, speak many languages and perform varied tasks. They exist on all levels of society. They have many things in common. Are you one of them? Let us define what slaves are and then you can discover any comparable areas of bondage in your life.

ONE: Slaves are forced to sever personal relationships. Their family can no longer be important to them. They must give up old friends. Personal ambition and initiative is squelched. Their personal values are surrendered. Submission is the deprecating status constantly imposed upon their lives.

When you choose to receive Christ as the Lord of your life, He does not impose demoralizing restrictions upon you. He does not require you to sever relationships with friends whom you cherish. Rather, He works with you and improves and grows each relationship into a positive situation where He can be honored — or, He grows you beyond the relationship.

For example: When a woman who is married receives Christ and is born again, Jesus does not interrupt that marriage relationship. Instead, He expresses His love for that woman's companion through her and draws the husband to Himself. The relationship is more beautiful than ever and Jesus becomes Lord of the man, of the woman and of the home.

Satan divides and severs relationships.

Jesus knits and heals relationships.

TWO: Slaves are forced to uproot and abandon what is treasured by them. They are taken where they do not choose to go and are required to do things which they do not want to do.

When those precious Africans were forcibly taken to America and sold into slavery, they lost all identity with their families and with their own heritage.

That is what Satan tries to achieve with the human race. He wants us to lose sight of our origin, our roots. We were created in the image of God. Satan wants to distort and destroy that image and sever our relationships as sons and daughters of the living God.

Satan wants to force you as a woman, to go where he chooses. He will attempt to oblige you to do things you would not want to do. He will reduce you to the level of his slave. How does he do this? He does his dirty work through people, through systems, through cultures, through traditions and ofttimes through *religion.*

Satan is a liar, a thief and a murderer. *He comes to steal, to kill and to destroy.*^{Jn.10:10} Satan always reduces human persons to a subordinate level.

When Jesus comes into your life, He raises you to His level. He protects your freedom. He works

115

through your will and your choices. He gives you His nature, His values, His priorities, His love and His patience. You learn to value yourself; you value other people. You honor your freedom; you honor the freedom of others. Then you begin to grasp life's greatest secret — the art of being a true servant, and the status of true *Self-Esteem*.

You cannot be a servant while doing the things others oblige you to do. That is being a slave. The Christian life is not a life of force but of favor.

Satan reduces you to slavery.

Jesus grows you to greatness.

Satan severs relationships.

Jesus develops them.

Satan takes away your choices

Jesus helps you make the right choices.

THREE: Slaves are forced to abandon personal dreams and desires. They cannot enjoy the things that make their lives happy and fulfilled. They must strive and toil for the happiness and fulfillment of another person.

Never abandon your own dreams. Your own ambitions in life, your personal goals are important. Commit yourself to seeing them realized. Never give up!

Anyone or any situation that requires you to

relinquish what is important to your happiness or that obliges you to sacrifice your dreams and desires has become your master.

Slavery is a dead-end trail.

Following Jesus, being His servant, His expression, makes life a journey that is exciting and fulfilling. He will grow you to greatness. And He defines *greatness* as being a servant — His kind of servant — one with true *Self-Esteem*.

FOUR: A slave must vacate the role of leadership. Satan wants to prevent you from ever being a leader. He wants you to be submissive at home, inactive in your community, silent in your church and unfulfilled in your life.

Slavery and leadership do not go together. Regardless of who you are, there is a place of leadership and of self-value for you. Jesus is your leader and He leads others through you in every facet of life.

As a servant of Jesus Christ, you are destined to be a leader among those whom you influence.

FIVE: From the moment you begin to be a slave, your spirit begins to expire. When your personal choice in any sphere of life is taken from you, you begin to die in that area. You have no reason for life when you have no right of choice.

Many marriages have failed and others are frozen because of male dominance in the relationship. Is there not room in a marriage for leadership both on the part of the husband and of the wife? When Christ is truly the Lord of your life, and the Head of your home, there will be beautiful harmony and warmth in your marriage. Love each other as Christ has loved you. Submit to one another and whatever you want your companion to do to you, do that to your companion. This is being the Jesus kind of servant.

But we must be allowed to make free choices in order to be able to serve people. As servants, we do as Jesus, the great Servant, did. We reach out to hurting people. They give us reason to live. A slave cannot reach out to people; they do only what they are required or allowed to do by their master.

To accept the yoke of slavery means to ...

1 - Sever your valued relationships;

2 - Surrender what is rightfully yours;

3 - Abandon your dreams, ambitions and desires;

4 - Vacate the role of leadership;

5 - Expire in your spirit.

The *Servant* Lifestyle

Now that we have a practical idea of what a slave is, we can look at the characteristics and the lifestyle of a servant.

FIRST: A servant is self-motivated and self-directed. A servant steers their own ship. A servant makes lots of decisions and choices.

When Jesus lives in you and you have chosen to let Him express His servitude in you, you will never need to be forced to do good things. You will do the same thing Jesus would do under similar circumstances. You will choose to do the same things Jesus did because His servant nature is in you.

The Night Visitor

One night while visiting a friend in the hospital, I met an elderly gentleman whose wife had just suffered a serious heart attack. They lived on a farm near a small town in Oklahoma. The nearest hospital with cardiac equipment was in the city of Tulsa. So he and his wife were rushed there in an ambulance. He sat by her all the way into the city which was about 40 miles. He had nowhere to go so he planned to sleep in a chair in the hospital lobby.

I was concerned about him. I thought of the nice guest bedroom T.L. and I had in our home. After visiting with the man for a few minutes, I invited him to go home with me. I promised to bring him back to the hospital early the next morning. He accepted my invitation. When we reached home, I presented my new friend to my husband. He was a bit surprised, but very loving and gentle with the man. He treated him as he would his own father. After a warm shower, some toast and hot chocolate, our friend fell asleep in our cozy bed, snuggled up in a pair of T.L.'s pajamas.

I never once thought of calling T.L. to see if he would allow me to bring the man home for the night. I am a servant of Jesus Christ and I was serving His will and His love by caring for that stranger in the name of my Lord.

You cannot be a servant if there is someone restricting you. You can only be a slave. If you want to give and you want to help the poor and to lift the fallen and to visit the sick, if there is someone who will punish you for what you have chosen to do, that is slavery.

You Cannot Serve Two Masters

SECOND: A servant exercises the gift of love. As a servant you do not need to search for loving things to do. It is your nature to love. Your nature is what you are and what you do as a result of your own desire and initiative. When Jesus lives in you, you are programmed to love and to serve people. That is *Leading By Serving,* and that produces *Women And Self-Esteem.*

When you are a Jesus person, you are not expected to neglect yourself. Religion may require you to put others first and to not think about yourself at all. But genuine love begins with yourself. When you love yourself, you can then love another person. When you value yourself, you are capable of valuing another person. When you respect yourself, you will demonstrate respect for another person. When you guard your own freedom, you can allow another person to be free. Include yourself in your love.

A servant — a Jesus woman, a Jesus man, loves people.

There is no weapon formed against you that can prosper.[Is.54:17] Why? Because you have the power of love. There is no weapon that can prosper or win against love. A true servant exercises this gift of love constantly and wonderful things happen as a result.

It may not always be easy to express love. But Jesus said: *Be perfect even as I am perfect.*[Mt.5:48] That is an awesome command. But the fact that Jesus said it means that we can eventually achieve His perfection. He is really saying, *Allow Me to be perfect in you.*

THIRD: A servant regards people as their principle reason for service, for ministry, for success, for achievement, for fulfillment and for *Self-Esteem.*

What can you achieve in life without people? You need people in order to succeed in any area of life. No matter how intelligent you are, you cannot exercise your knowledge without people. People are important to God. People are important to you. People are important to a servant.

Even God cannot accomplish His dream without people.

When you regard people as your main channel for service to God, you do not see the color, the race, the gender or the social status of individuals. You see the person.

There is no prejudice in the true servant.

FOURTH: A servant values a human person, starting with one's own self. Because you value yourself, you can become a servant to others because you value them too. As a woman, you cannot be a servant, the kind Jesus talks about, without having very good *Self-Esteem.*

God values you so much that He gave His only Son to die for your sins. Jesus valued you so much that He gave His life so that you can be saved. *Mk.10:45*

Can you value yourself as a woman, enough to be a servant, a physical expression of Jesus to humankind?

God needs you. He does not need gold mines. He does not need diamonds. He has no need for pearls. But God does need you. The expressions of wealth, such as gold and diamonds are for your pleasure, but God's pleasure is in *you*. You are worth more than all of the diamonds and all of the gold in the world.

FIFTH: A servant awakens abilities in other people. A true servant is really a leader. That is why a servant arouses talents and inspires abilities in others. A leader is also a teacher. And the art of teaching is the ability to spark in a student the desire to learn.

A servant, a leader, a teacher never demeans another human person. A servant never feels superior to others, never looks on others as though they are inferior and without value. Sharp, critical, negative words never come from a true servant's lips.

SIXTH: A servant never neglects a responsibility or duty. As a servant you give every task 100% of your ability. You see a responsibility as your human response to God's ability within you.

Practice responding to human needs when you confront them. The only way God can meet those needs is through a human person. Let that person be you. Choose to be a servant and achieve true greatness with valid *Self-Esteem*.

SEVENTH: A servant treasures identity with Jesus Christ who was the greatest servant humankind has ever known.

Perhaps the best formula for a servant attitude, while refusing the slave mentality, was given by Jesus Himself. The principle of self-dignity, and the individual right of choice are graphically endorsed in these words of Jesus.

*If you are forced to go one mile, go two.*Mt.5:41-48

If you do only what you are forced to do, you are yielding to a slave attitude. But just as soon as you choose to go the second mile, *you* become the leader; you take command of the task to be performed and you rise to the servant status and to true *Self-Esteem*. By that choice, you become the leader of the one who wanted to be your master.

The command imposed upon you disregarded your choice. That is slavery. But when you went beyond what was demanded, you wielded your right of choice. You stepped up from slavery into the dignified status of a servant. That choice made you a master in the very situation that was contrived to demean you.

Jesus said: *If you are slapped on one cheek; turn the other also.*Lu.6:29

He was not advocating physical abuse for women. Prior to this statement Jesus had said: *Listen all of you. Love your enemies. Do good to those who hate you. Pray for the happiness of those who curse you; implore God's blessing on those who hurt you.* Lu.6:27-28

Jesus was teaching about the attitude of believers, the nature of His disciples, the character of a servant, of your identity with Him.

If you are dealt a blow, criticized, hurt or misjudged, do not react as a slave. Do not cower and be intimidated. Rather, remember who you are. Treasure your identity with Christ and appear as though nothing ever happened. Turn your fresh, uninjured self toward your offender. You then rise from the status of a slave to become the leader, the forgiver, the servant. That is *Leading By Serving.*

A meek Christian woman is not a weak Christian woman. A gentle woman who is a follower of Christ is a Jesus woman. Jesus was both strong and gentle. When you are like Him, you are too.

Jesus said: *If you are ordered to court, and your shirt (or dress) is taken from you, give your coat too.* Mt.5:4

If people persecute you and take what you possess, you can seize the initiative, make a choice and give them something extra. When you surrender only what is demanded, you are a slave. When you choose to give more than is demanded, you become a servant with true *Self-Esteem.* Be a giver. Meet a human need. Be a servant.

Remember: A slave has no choice. A slave cannot pursue an idea. A slave cannot be creative. A slave can take no initiative.

Satan's strategy is to steal a woman's creativity, her originality, her uniqueness, her initiative and ultimately her life. He makes her afraid. He wants her to fear making a decision. He wants her to be so demeaned that she does not dare to do something new and different. He calls her a fool for thinking a new thought.

Do not be afraid of him. He is just the devil, and Jesus has broken his power over you.

Jesus always gives you choices. He offers you options. He gives you creative ability. He gives you initiative. He trusts you with His nature. He gifts you with originality. He renews your confidence. He grows you to be like Him.

Satan gives you fear; Jesus gives you faith.

Satan gives you hatred; Jesus gives you love.

Satan gives you poverty; Jesus gives you prosperity.

Satan gives you sickness; Jesus gives you health.

Satan gives you enemies; Jesus gives you friends.

Do you want to be great in the Kingdom of God? Your greatness begins right where you are. Grow as a servant, the Jesus kind of servant. That is the greatest accomplishment that you can realize in life. It is the discovery of *Leading By Serving*. It is the true secret for *Women And Self-Esteem*.

Nothing can force you to become a slave, unless you yourself surrender to slavery. Your religion cannot; your culture cannot; your spouse cannot. Only your own pattern of thoughts can reduce you to the role of a slave.

People will esteem you on the same level that you esteem yourself. And you exhibit your own level of self-esteem by your pattern of thoughts, your words, your actions, and your form of relationships.

Whatever you do, do it with a servant's mind and heart. You will be astonished at the change this will bring to your life as a woman follower of Christ.

A slave does what is expected of him or her by others.

A servant takes the initiative and makes choices.

A slave is bound and limited.

A servant is free, unrestricted and has no limits.

A servant is ...

1 - Self-motivated and self-directed;

2 - Exercises the gift of love;

3 - Regards people as the principle reason for service and ministry;

4 - Values each human person,

5 - Awakens abilities in other people;

6 - Never neglects an opportunity for service;

7 - Treasures her or his identity with Jesus Christ.

You were bought at a price; do not become slaves of human beings. [1Co.7:23 NEB]

You have been given freedom: not freedom to do wrong, but freedom to love and serve each other. [Ga.5:13]

Whether one–by–one, group–by–group, or nation–by–nation, the multi-national gospel ministry of Daisy inspires women, as well as men, to discover true dignity, peace and happiness in the non-judgmental role of Christ's love–representatives in life. Here she shares with university students on the steps of the Buddhist Marble Temple in Bangkok.

Panoramic views of the T. L. and Daisy Stadium field. (Center) National Women's encouragement to the thousands of women powerful message preached by Dr. Daisy.

Osborn Crusade at Mombasa's Municipal
Miracle Day — an overwhelming
whose lives are transformed by the

Daisy teaches thousands of African women during her National Women's Ministry Seminar in Kenya's Nyanza province.

Daisy Osborn conducts a National Women's mass meeting at Kampala, with over 200,000 women in attendance—besides men and children.

Daisy conducts a National Women's Conference at Accra, Ghana.

WOMEN'S NATIONAL CONFERENCE — E. AFRICA

Daisy Osborn seeds the women of the world
in her national women's mass rallies abroad.

INDONESIAN WOMEN'S DAY — SURABAJA

WOMEN'S NATIONAL MIRACLE DAY — KAMPALA

AUSTRALIAN CONFERENCE

Daisy proclaims the gospel at Municipal Stadium in Surabaya, Java, (Below) Osborn daughter, LaDonna, pastor of International Gospel Center at Tulsa, OK, preaches Christ at stadium in Papua New Guinea.

After Daisy's powerful message, call to accept Christ, and prayer for the sick, a blind woman receives sight (center) and a crippled man (below) is totally healed as he receives Christ in Surabaya.

T.L. AND DAISY OSBORN CRUSADES

AFRICA

S. AMERICA

INDONESIA

CARIBBEAN

PHILIPPINES

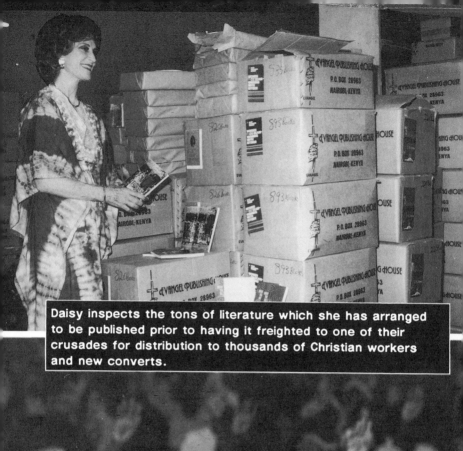

Daisy inspects the tons of literature which she has arranged to be published prior to having it freighted to one of their crusades for distribution to thousands of Christian workers and new converts.

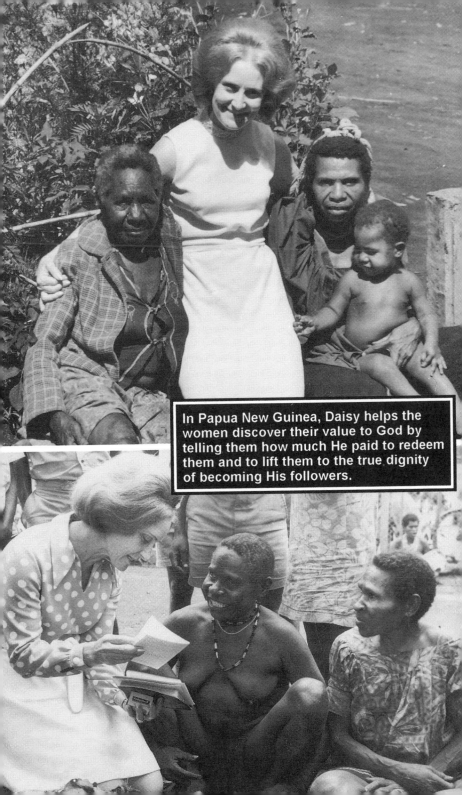

In Papua New Guinea, Daisy helps the women discover their value to God by telling them how much He paid to redeem them and to lift them to the true dignity of becoming His followers.

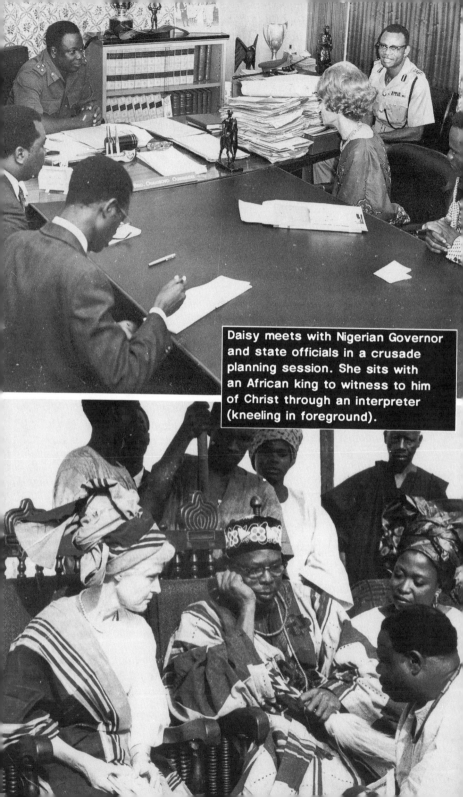

Daisy meets with Nigerian Governor and state officials in a crusade planning session. She sits with an African king to witness to him of Christ through an interpreter (kneeling in foreground).

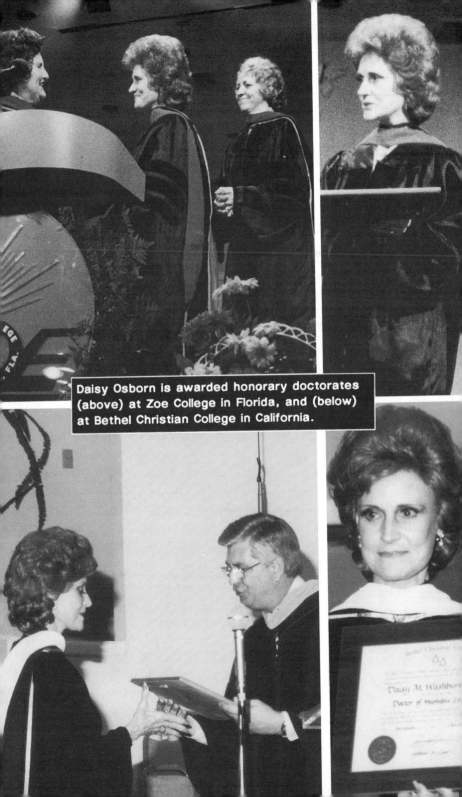

Daisy Osborn is awarded honorary doctorates (above) at Zoe College in Florida, and (below) at Bethel Christian College in California.

Daisy Osborn shares with her husband, T.L., in ministering the love of Christ to nations around the world. She has never been limited by her gender anymore than by her race. They both believe that Christ in a woman is no different than He is in a man. Here, they rejoice together on the final day of another triumphant crusade of evangelism.

V

LIFE
WITH
PURPOSE

TODAY YOU WILL get a close-up view of what can happen to you when you, as a woman, learn to see *God* and *others* and *yourself,* with a new attitude of human-value.

What do you ponder most when you think about God? What is your attitude about others? How do you regard yourself as a woman? How does God see you?

Every woman must learn to see herself as God sees her, and to believe in herself like God believes in her; she must think of herself as God thinks of her and confess what He says about her, instead of what traditional theology may have programmed her to believe.

God has paid a supreme price for you. You are somebody. You are loved and you are important. God believes in you. You are part of His plan. You as a woman, are unique — the only one of *you* that God has.

There is new life in Christ — not condemnation. There is salvation in Him — not slavery to religion, not guilt. There is deliverance in Him — not captivity. Our message must not wound but heal. To represent Christ, we cannot destroy. We must give life and joy and peace.

Chapter 5

LIFE WITH PURPOSE

THE THEME OF this chapter is to help you as a woman, to grasp a fresh perspective of life from God's standpoint of high esteem for humankind.

Here are some Bible verses that express some of what God says about a woman-believer in the New Testament:

So, now ... we have been made right in God's sight ... because of what Jesus Christ our Lord has done for us ... .

He has brought us into this place of highest privilege where we now stand, and we confidently and joyfully look forward to actually becoming all that God has had in mind for us to be ... .

We are able to hold our heads high ... for we know how dearly God loves us ... .

Now we rejoice in our wonderful new relationship with God — all because of what our Lord Jesus Christ has done in dying for our sins — making us friends of

God. *Ro.5:1,2,5,11 LB*

Remember these three statements:

vs.1 — *He has brought us to this place of highest privilege.*

vs.2 — *We joyfully look forward to becoming all that God has in mind for us to be.*

vs.11 — *We rejoice in our wonderful new relationship — making us friends of God.*

What marvelous and uplifting concepts and ideals these are, and how vital they are in the building of *Women And Self-Esteem!*

Today you will get a close-up view of what can happen to you as a woman believer, when you learn to see *God* and *others* and *yourself,* with a new attitude of human-value.

* * *

PART I

HOW YOU SEE *GOD*

FIRST: What do you ponder most when you think about God?

There are three important facts about Him that I urge you to never forget:

1. The fact that God is All Powerful!

2. The fact that He is Good!

3. The fact that He is Present with you now!

1st — God Is Powerful

What about His power?

One day Elisha was surrounded by enemies. But God sent horses and chariots of fire to deliver him,[2K.6:17] and the enemy fled. He does that today for women who trust in Him the same as He does for men of faith like Elisha.

A pagan chief and his men surrounded a pastor's house to kill him, but they saw big, strong guards around the house. Finally the chief accepted Christ and confessed his plot to kill the pastor.

Weeks later he told the pastor, *Since I've been a Christian your guards have all gone. Where are they? Where did they come from? I want to thank them for preventing me from killing God's messenger.*

Then the national pastor knew that God had sent His angels to protect him like He did for Elisha, because he had never had guards around his house.

Our God has not changed. His power is as real today as it ever was, and it is for women the same as it is for men. *Behold, I am the Lord, the God of all flesh: is there anything too hard for me?* Je.32:27

When Elisha, the prophet, died, his body was placed in a sepulchre. Then, later, another man died and was placed there too. The Bible says: *And as soon as the body touched Elisha's bones, the dead man revived and jumped to his feet.* 2K.13:21

That power is still real today!

A miracle similar to that happened in our Crusade in Calabar, Nigeria. They carried a dead man onto the platform where T.L, my husband, and I had preached under a mighty anointing.

Many miracles had happened, and the people had given witness to the healing wonders which they had received that night — right there where we had been preaching. When the man's dead body was laid there where God's power had been manifested in such a great way, suddenly the man sat up and was restored to life. It astounded everybody, and hundreds accepted Christ as a result. You see, God's Power is unchanged today.

2nd — God Is Good

But ... what good is a powerful God for a woman, if He is not a good God?

Our Lord sent Jesus to show us that He is not only powerful, but that He is good, that He is a Savior, a Healer, a Life-giver. And He never showed any difference in His regard for a woman or for a man.

John said: *As many as received Him, to them gave He power to become the children of God.*Jn.1:12 And Mark said: *As many as touched Him were made whole.*Mk.6:56 No one ever called on Him and was refused — no woman, or no man.

The Togo Villager

A dear village man came to one of our crusades in Togo. He had a terrible rupture, and one leg was lame. The first night he came, Jesus made him ever whit whole. Then he brought his daughter who was crippled from polio and could not walk, and she too was miraculously healed.

Then the old man brought his sister. She was kept chained to a tree like a wild animal because she was crazy. Four men helped him bring her to the crusade. The demons went out of her and she was perfectly restored. The whole family became faithful followers of Jesus. They saw that God is *good!*

God's Will For You Is GOOD!

I believe that every woman must come to understand that Satan is bad. God is good. Sickness is bad. Health is good. Failure is bad. Success is good. God's will for you as a woman, is *good.*

The Bible says: *I wish above all things that you may prosper and be in health, even as your soul prospers.*[3Jn.2] That applies to women the same as it does to men.

The Bible says: *No good thing will He withhold from them who walk uprightly.*[Ps.84:11]

3rd – God Is Present

Here is another aspect of our Lord that every woman must embrace: He is not only powerful and good, but He is *present!* He is by my side and by your side! Jesus said, *Lo, I am with you always, even unto the end of the world.*[Mt.28:20] He confirms His women-witnesses the same as He does His men-witnesses

In one of our crusades in India a young arrogant student stood at the back of the crowd with folded arms, seething in anger. He wondered what he could do to drive my husband and me out of town, because he despised our teaching about Jesus Christ.

But as we taught the people and then prayed, suddenly the Lord appeared to that young political activist. As Jesus looked straight into the young man's eyes, He opened His nail-pierced hands and said, *Behold My hands! I am Jesus!* Then with a soft smile and eyes of compassion, He disappeared.

The young man fell to his knees weeping, and right there, he received Jesus Christ as Lord and Master. He told the whole multitude what had happened to him and, as a result, hundreds accepted the Lord. That man saw the Lord and his life was changed forever.

God Is Present NOW!

Thank God, I as a woman have discovered that Jesus is unchanged today ... and *He is present, now*! I hope you can have a new look at Him; then, *nothing shall be impossible to you* [Mt.17:20] as a woman.

Stephen, a man of faith in the Bible, was being stoned to death for his witness of Jesus Christ. Then the Bible says, he looked up and he saw *Jesus standing at the right hand of God.* [Ac.7:56] Stephen had a new vision of Jesus and his tragedy turned into triumph!

So that is why I say: Every woman needs a fresh look at God, to see that He is *all powerful,* then that He is *good* and compassionate, and finally that He is *present* with us. He is the *Great I AM.* Ponder these facts when you as a woman, think about God.

* * *

PART 2

HOW YOU SEE *OTHERS*

THE SECOND VITAL viewpoint that each woman-believer needs to consider is: What is your attitude about *others?*

Here are three statements about *others* that can affect your regard for them from this day forward:

1. See that *others* comprise the finest purpose of your own life as a woman.

2. See that *others* provide the only way to really express your faith in God.

3. See that serving *others* is the master key to your own unlimited success in a real *Life With Purpose.*

Now we shall review some Bible verses that validate those thoughts and that put them into clear focus for women as believers and as followers of Christ.

1st – Others And Purpose

See that others comprise the finest purpose of your own life as a woman.

Jesus was the perfect example of God's ideal for us as women, the same as for men. He taught one simple rule for life:

Love ONE ANOTHER; as I have loved you. Jn.13:34 *Whatever you desire that others do to you, do that to them.*Mt.7:12 *Whoever wants to be the greatest of all must be the servant OF ALL.*Mk.10:44 LB

*But when He (Jesus) saw the multitudes, He was moved with compassion on them ... then He said to His disciples, The harvest truly is plenteous, but the laborers are few.*Mt.9:36-37

He is saying to us: *The people are there! They are ripe! They will believe! They will respond and be blessed! But I need a person to love them through! I need you! Can I love them through you? Can I heal them through you? Can I bring them peace and tranquility through you?*

We are talking about our attitude toward *others.* They constitute our finest purpose in living.

2nd – Others And Faith

See that others provide the only way to express your faith in God.

Jesus said, *I was hungry, and you gave Me meat: I was thirsty, and you gave Me drink: I was a stranger, and you took Me in: Naked, and you clothed Me: I was sick, and you visited Me: I was in prison, and you came to Me.*Mt.25:35-36

Then He said: *Inasmuch as you have done it unto one of the least of these, you have done it unto Me.*[Mt.25:40] That is why I say, see that *others* provide the only way to express our faith in God.

If we want to really discover Jesus Christ, we will not find Him in the holy sanctuaries, but in the prison houses, among the sick, the naked, the needy. We can serve Christ only as we serve them.

Porno Theater Becomes Gospel Center

A young woman was saved in New York City, and has since become a great soulwinner. She had been a chemical dependant and a prostitute. As a result of a gang fight, one of her arms had to be amputated, and she wears a prosthesis.

There were three pornographic cinemas, side by side, in a New York ghetto. The middle one was for sale. The money was raised by Christians who bought it and started Gospel meetings. Opposite the entrance are three hotels which are managed by professional pimps for their prostitutes and prostitutors.

That young woman — herself a reformed prostitute and converted chemical dependent — chose that place to begin a new work for God. She has God's viewpoint of life — and of others. She knows that she can only love and serve God by loving and serving *others.*

Before long, several hundred people were attending church there. Instead of condemning the cancer of sin in that ghetto, that group of soul-winners moved in and started curing that cancer. They demonstrated true Christian faith in action — by serving *others*.

You see, that is the only way to really express our faith in God. What we do to *others*, we do to Him. Real active faith is not what is expressed in beautiful rituals in the sanctuary, but it is what is expressed in beautiful deeds and actions out among the people who are in need.

We Solved Problems

I heard a young pastor of one of America's large churches say: *Some years ago we came into this city with nothing. We did not expect people to come to us. We knew we had to go to them.*

He said, *We never left the area for eighteen months. Every day, from morning until night, my wife and I knocked on doors, visited prisons, ministered in hospitals and houses and got people saved, out where they live and work and suffer and die.*

Then they acquired old buses and hauled hundreds of children from the ghettos, the slums, and the poorest areas, to their church. He said, *We went to the people who had problems.* After a few years between one and two thousand attend each service at that church.

Many of those formerly destitute families, former prostitutes, prisoners and drunkards, are today owners of businesses and honorable citizens.

They have produced a small army of workers who are soulwinners throughout the city and area.

Senators, doctors and lawyers attend that church now, and it is a powerful community of believers for God's work.

That husband-wife pastoral team knows the secret. They see in those who are hungry and thirsty, in the orphans, the prisoners, the naked, the sick and the suffering, the only place where they can really express their Christian faith in action.

The Bible says, *faith ... works by love.*[Ga.5:6]

John asks: *Whoever does not love their brother or sister who they have seen, how can they love God whom they have not seen?* [1Jn.4:20]

So to love God is to love others — *Let us not love in word, neither in tongue, (as John said), but in DEED and in truth.*[1Jn.3:18]

He asks: How can we as women, talk about loving God, or serving God, or expressing our faith in God, if we know people who are in need, and if we do nothing about it? [1Jn.3:17]

As women-followers of Christ and as His co-workers, we can only express our real faith as we act with real love toward others. Jesus is wherever there are people in need. The way we respond to them, is the way we respond to Him. That is why I say, We must see that *others* provide the only way to really express our faith in God — the only way to really serve God.

3rd — Others And Success

See that serving *others* is the master key to your own unlimited success in a real *Life With Purpose.*

As women-believers we can only succeed as we help others to succeed.

Jesus said, *Give, and it shall be given unto you; good measure, pressed down, and shaken together, and running over, shall others give into your bosom.*[Lu.6:38] He means — whatever you give, more of it shall be given to you.

Paul said: *Whatever anyone sows, that shall they also reap.*[Ga.6:7] The kind of seed you sow in others is the kind of life you reap for yourself.

Jesus' rule was: *All things whatever you desire that others should do to you, do the same to them.*[Mt.7:12] This means: whatever you do to others you will reap from others.

Jesus said that we are to be seed-planters. He said: *The seed is the word.*[Lu.8:11] And the *field is the world*[Mt.13:38] — the world of people around us.

Open Your Heart To Others — You'll Never Be Lonely!

Plant kindness in people and you will reap kindness. Heal people by planting seeds of love and kindness in their lives, and you will reap healing love and kindness from others. Hate people and you will be hated. Envy people and you will be envied.

Open your door, your heart and your ears to others, and you will never be lonely.

> Jesus showed us God by what He did for others. We show our faith in God by what we do for others.

> Jesus showed us God by what happened to people who came in contact with Him. We show what God is like in our lives by what happens to people who come into contact with us.

> You grow as you help others grow. You prosper as you help others prosper.

> You learn by teaching. You gain by giving. You reap by planting. You receive by giving.

You see, as the songwriter said:

> *A bell is not a bell 'til you ring it;*
> *A song is not a song 'til you sing it.*
> *Love in your heart is not put there to stay;*
> *Love is not love 'til you give it away.*

Love Is Action

So, as a woman, take a new look at *others* today. *Lift up your eyes, and look on the fields.*[Jn.4:35]

Find a need and meet it.

Find a hurt and heal it.

Find a problem and solve it.

Find someone who is down and lift them up.

It is as you reach out to others that God reaches out to you.

It is when you bless others that God blesses you.

So think that way when you look at *others*. Plant in them what you want to reap in your own life. You are the master of your own harvest. Just plant in others the kind of seed you want to reap, and God will fulfill your greatest dreams. You will find yourself among the valued corps of *Women And Self-Esteem.*

We have talked about a woman's attitude toward *God.* Then we have discussed her attitude toward *others.*

* * *

PART 3

HOW YOU SEE *YOURSELF*

NOW, AS A WOMAN, what is your real attitude about *yourself?* How does God see *you?*

You are created in God's image, to have His nature, to share His plan, to think His thoughts, to be a winner, to succeed, to be happy, to prosper. That is the life God created *you* for.

Never allow religious indoctrinazation and cultural brainwashing to cause you to demean yourself as an inferior creature. That is nothing less than pernicious self-destruction. Never beat yourself over the head with accusing, negative thoughts and confessions. No one has the right to destroy or to disparage what God has created in His own image, to walk and to talk with Him and — that includes every woman.

The Bible clearly teaches that we should each come to God in repentance, and confess our sins to Him, covering nothing before Him. Then He promises to forgive us and to receive us as His child, and to make us a new creature in Christ Jesus [Ac.2:38; 1Jn.1:9; Jn.1:12] — a valued member of His own Royal Family. That acceptance into His family is not qualified by our human gender. Never forget that.

But after we have come into God's family and

have been received as His children, we are not to go through life as Christians, confessing that we are weak, rebellious, unworthy, sinning worms of the dust. Once we have been converted, we have become the sons and the daughters of God. We belong to His family. We are re-created in His image. We are born again. We have His nature.*Eph.2:19*

The coming of Jesus Christ and the Good News has brought to us a new and positive message — of a new creation, a new birth, a new life, a new nature, a new way. *If any one* (man or woman) *be in Christ, he or she is a new creature: old things are passed away; behold, all things are become new.*²*Co.5:17*

The new birth is the same miracle for women that it is for men. When we come to Christ, we are made new. We are changed. Believe in that change. Think about that change. Confess it. Sing about it. Act like you have been changed — once you turn from sin and embrace Jesus Christ as your Lord.

As a woman-disciple of Christ, never condemn yourself; then you will never condemn others. Start believing in yourself, then you will start believing in others.

I See You! I See Me!

Out on the western plains of America, a new immigrant family arrived in a frontier town. They halted their wagon by a farmer's house and asked: *What kind of people live around here?*

The farmer said, *Well newcomer, what kind of people lived in the old country where you came from?*

Oh, the immigrant replied, *It was terrible. There were crooks and liars, deceivers and dishonest people everywhere. The business people were crooked and the officials were worse. That's why we left that place, to find a new world where life can be better.*

Well, the farmer said, *I expect that's the kind of people you'll find around here too.*

Later, another load of immigrants arrived and stopped to talk with the farmer. They too wanted to know what kind of people had settled in that area.

The wise farmer asked, *Well, newcomer, what kind of people lived in the old country where you came from?*

Oh, the immigrant replied, *It was a fine land. We had good neighbors. Our merchants were honorable. Our people cared for each other. It was hard to leave them, but we thought we could bring some of our good out west to help to build this great new nation!*

Well, sir, said the farmer, *You're going to be mighty happy here. I think you'll find that same kind of people here.*

As women, we must realize that we see in others what we see in ourselves. A woman who does not trust others, is not trustworthy. If she believes she is bad, she will believe that others are bad. If she suspicions dishonesty in others, it is a sign that she needs to re-examine her own character and life.

Once a woman discovers who she really is in Christ, she can stop condemning others. When any woman disparages and discredits others, she is only announcing what she thinks about her own self as a person.

What We Teach Worldwide

In our great Soulwinning Institutes overseas, we gather thousands of Christian men and women preachers and workers, and we teach them for two hours, three times a day.

Where do we begin? With these six facts of the New Christ life which are so vital to both women and men involved in God's work:

* God is what He says He is.

* I am what He says I am.

* God has what He says He has.

* I have what He says I have.

* God will do what He says He will do.

* I can do what He says I can do.

165

T.L., my husband, and I start at the New Birth, and focus on the miracle transformation of our old natures to the new Jesus life.

We emphasize that each woman as well as each man must learn to see themselves as God sees them, and to believe in themselves like God believes in them; that each one must think of themselves as God thinks of them, and confess what He says about them instead of what traditional theology may have programmed them to believe about themselves.

Demean Or Esteem

The pastor of the great Crystal Cathedral in California is a remarkable Christian leader who constantly advocates what he calls *Possibility Thinking* — or positive believing — or faith.

The church services, and the pastoral messages are beamed into homes all across America and around the world, every Sunday morning. It is positive. People are lifted. Thousands are influenced to believe in Christ. Every message is a challenge to fresh possibilities in the new life of Christ. Never is there condemnation. Always there is faith, hope and love.

Wherever a woman or a man pastor gives that kind of gospel message, it always lifts people and the crowds will seek out any church like that where they can come and be blessed. The world has enough problems and hurts without getting more from the pulpit.

Christ did not come to condemn people, but to love and bless and save them. The most devastating effect upon the human spirit is negative, ugly, condemning thoughts and words. Sometimes it is called humility, but in reality, it is self-destruction.[Lu.19:10; Jn.3:17]

No woman and no man has the right to stand in a pulpit or before a class and fill the minds of people with negative, unpleasant phrases and pronouncements that destroy enthusiasm with ugly, negative concepts of human persons.

Jesus condemned no one — not even the woman and the man taken in adultery, nor the thief on the Cross. And as His ambassadors, we must not condemn people either.[Lu.23:39-42; 2Co.5:20]

There is new life in Christ — not condemnation. There is salvation in Him — not slavery to religion, not guilt. There is deliverance in Him — not captivity. Our message must not wound but heal. To represent Christ, we cannot destroy. We must give life and joy and peace.

The Reached — The Unreached

The great problem every messenger of Christ faces is to communicate the Gospel of Jesus Christ to the unconverted without offending those who are converted by methods or vocabulary which does not seem *religious* enough.

You see — Christianity is not to be morbid and depressing. It is the Good News that we have been redeemed; that anyone can now rise and walk again with God; that the worst person has unlimited possibilities; that people can become new creatures. Does that sound negative or gloomy? No. That is the doorway to a new kind of *Life With Purpose* for women as well as for men.

As women believers, we must upgrade our prayers, our confessions, our sermons and our songs. The Crystal Cathedral pastor has edited many of the old church hymns which are used in worship there.

The self-condemning lines have been replaced by phrases of faith and new living. The struggling thoughts have been changed to concepts of victory in Christ. The verses that express negativism now radiate positive ideals. They have kept the familiar music but have changed the words to lift, enliven and inspire Christians to go out and to succeed in life.

Faith Statements

Here are seven statements about yourself which I hope you, as a woman or a man, will engrave in your mind; rehearse them in your ears when you lie down and when you rise up.

Fix them as mottos before you in your house or office or shop. Pray that pastors and leaders will capture these ideas and make them the new theme of their teaching. Write them into new songs. Memorize them. Repeat them before you go to sleep and as soon as you awaken — until they become a part of your self-image as a woman or as a man.

No. 1. I am created in God's likeness!

No. 2. I am unique — one of a kind!

No. 3. I am of infinite value — to God and to others!

No. 4. I am loved, in spite of my faults!

No. 5. I am redeemed and accepted by the Lord!

No. 6. I am empowered for His divine blessings to serve others!

No. 7. I am commissioned as an Ambassador in His Royal Kingdom!

That is *Life With Purpose.*

You are somebody. You are loved and you are important. God believes in you. You are part of His plan. You are unique — the only one of *you* that God has.

Say it and think it, pray it and sing it until you actually believe it. When you do, you will enroll yourself among the ever-increasing worldwide corps of distinguished *Women And Self-Esteem.*

The Poison Of Negative Words

A poor girl from Europe recently ran away from home and traveled across the ocean to Tulsa, Oklahoma, just to talk to T.L. and me.

From childhood, her parents had told her that she was stupid, that she could not learn, that she was unattractive, that she could never get a job, that she could never attract a husband. The more they said those things, the more they tattooed her subconscious, and the more she acted out the part. (It is exactly the way that women in church classes or as church members become what their teachers or pastors talk about.)

This lady had always lived at home where she was dominated by this negative, destructive atmosphere. She became insecure, timid, withdrawn, and demoralized. Her father and mother had succeeded in making a slave of their own daughter — simply by planting negative, destructive seeds in her mind. She was afraid to go out on the street alone. The only work she ever did was scrubbing floors.

If she had been as stupid as her parents told her she was, she never would have secretly pondered a trip to America — to see Daisy and T.L. Osborn. She had to secretly get her own passport and visa

170

and arrange for her own air ticket. That took a bit of doing on her part.

She was not stupid. She was just emotionally starved and mentally devastated by cruel parents who were transferring their own self-hatred to the closest victim they could reach — their own daughter.

Words Are Seed-Power

If you teach a Bible class, if you are an exhorter, a pastor, an evangelist, a parent, a leader — woman or man, never forget the power and the influence of the words which you plant in the minds of your listeners. Whether they are positive or negative, they are seeds. And they will produce, in your listeners, the type of people that you yourself have engendered by your own words.

If you make a habit of talking about judgment and condemnation, you will produce those who judge and condemn you in return — the inevitable harvest of your own seed-planting.

If you pronounce criticism toward others, you will predestine yourself to reap the kind of people who will eventually rise and criticize you in return.

But if you occupy yourself with subjects of love, the pardon of Christ, His compassion, His longsuffering, then you will reap the virtues of love, pardon, compassion and longsuffering.

Whatever you sow in your class, your congregation or in the minds of your loved ones at your house, never forget that you will reap what your words and your attitude have sown in people. It is impossible to avoid the results of that law. It's process is as irreversible for women as it is for men.

New Words — New Life

We took that young European lady into our private prayer chamber, and as we showed her love and esteem and compassion, we could see that behind her emotionally scarred face was a brilliant, lovely lady who wanted to be somebody in life. Actually she was extremely perceptive. She grasped statements that lifted her self-esteem like a drowning person grabs a straw.

Her mouth and face twitched and grimaced as she talked. Her head and shoulders twisted involuntarily. Her whole body reflected her demoralized emotional state. Almost anyone would have thought she was a neurotic and emotionally unbalanced person; yet her only problem was the ugly negative words and thoughts with which she had been so perniciously impregnated.

Positive Power

That young woman stood in our prayer chamber looking up to God. As tears rolled down her cheeks, we asked her to confess these things out loud:

I am created in God's likeness. I am somebody important in God's eyes. He believes in me. He paid a price for me. He wants me and needs me. I am part of His plan. God loves me as much as He loves anyone else.

Then we prayed with her, and when she returned to Europe, she was a new woman. She believed that she had a *Life With Purpose*, that she could succeed in life.

She was thinking positive thoughts about herself, walking more uprightly, with her shoulders straighter. She could smile. She had hope. She had a new outlook. Her whole life would change because her thoughts were changed. She was joining the rising ranks of *Women And Self-Esteem.*

The Battered Penny

Just before she returned to Europe, T.L. and I were jogging alongside the river in Tulsa, when T.L. saw on the pavement a battered, beaten penny. It was so scarred by the hundreds of cars that had rolled over it that one could hardly recognize that it was a penny.

T.L. picked it up and as he held it in his hand, he told me that the Lord whispered to him: *That coin is worth as much as a beautiful shiny penny. It's value is the same. It is like that dear lady from Europe.*

Go tell her what I have said to you. Though she is scarred and battered by her parents and acquaintances, tell her that she is as valuable as the most beautiful lady in Europe.

We took that coin and placed it in her hands and while she looked at it, T.L. gave her God's message. Then while she held it, she repeated after him:

My life is like this battered coin. But I am as valuable as the most perfect and beautiful person in Europe!

She promised to keep that coin with her Bible. Every time anyone would say anything derogatory to her, she promised us that she would hold that battered coin and say: *My life is like this battered coin. But I am as valuable as the most beautiful person in Europe.*

It has been miraculous, what a change has taken place in her life.

Kariuki, The Insane Beggar

A poor insane maniac was brought to one of our crusades. His hair was full of fleas. His body was filthy. His eyes were wild. His clothes were rags that barely covered his nakedness.

For seventeen years he had been a lunatic, living on the roads and in the forest, like an animal.

That day at our crusade, Jesus came into his life. The demons went out of him and he was normal. What a kind and gentle man he became. He wept as he told how demons had tormented him.

There on the platform, T.L. put his arms around that dirty, stinking, pitiful looking man and told him: *Kariuki, you are my brother now. We are in God's family together. We have the same Father. You are created in God's image, just as much as me. You are important to Him. He loves you. He needs you. You are a chosen vessel for God's work. He has a plan for your life that no one else can fulfill* [2Ti.2:21; Ep.2:10]

What a change had been wrought. Now he was somebody important! He belonged to the King of Kings and Lord of Lords.

We told the pastors to take him where he could have a hot bath, to disinfect his head, to get his hair cut, and to buy him new clothes and shoes and a necktie.

When he returned the next day, we hardly recognized him. Already the seed-thoughts we had planted in him had begun to affect his attitude.

T.L. asked him to read the scripture lesson before he preached. Kariuki did it beautifully. We were so proud of him. Imagine how God felt about him. He had paid the supreme price to redeem him.

Each day Kariuki gave His witness. He wanted to talk to everyone about Jesus. He got a good job. Now he is serving the Lord. His life is a living example of God's love and value of human persons, and of real *Life With Purpose.*

Kariuki was fortunate. As soon as he was saved and delivered from demons, he heard positive thoughts about himself, ideals that lifted him.

He was told that he was created in God's image, to be part of God's plan; that he was loved; that he was important; that he could succeed. He grasped God's opinion of himself. He discovered *Life With Purpose.*

You Are Loved — As You Are

It is vital that you as a woman, realize that God paid a supreme price for you too — the blood and life of His only begotten Son, Jesus Christ. He would never pay such a price for a nobody. He would only pay such a price for a somebody. You are God's prize! You are valuable in God's divine plan.

You may have lived sinfully. But remember that Jesus Christ only saves sinners. God's pardon is only for those who have done wrong. God's redemption is only for those who are lost. God's salvation is only for people who are not what they could have been.

Jesus welcomes you and loves you like you are.

When you look at the price that God paid for you, then you will say: *I must be important!* Your self-esteem will increase. You will begin to love God who loved you, and that will cause you to love others. Love is God at work within you. The Bible says: *(You) can do all things through Christ who strengthens (you).*[Ph.4:13] His strength in you is His love at work within you. And that is the greatest power on earth for any woman or for any man.

Because as a woman, you embrace God's opinion of yourself, you will no longer want to destroy the wonderful person that God made in you. You will value your body, your mind, your lungs, your organs, your blood, your heart. Since He accepts you, you can accept yourself and you will begin to accept others.

You will speak for Him and salvation will come to lost souls. You will pray to Him and wonderful changes will happen to people. You will touch the sick and needy and His wonderful power will heal them.

Your body becomes His temple. You are authorized to act on His behalf. You are part of

God's plan to bless and heal and help and lift people. This never depends on your gender.

No Hands But Yours

During the second world war, a beautiful statue of Jesus, in France, was damaged. The villagers there loved their church and they lovingly gathered up the pieces of their statue which had stood in front of their church, and they repaired it. But they never found the hands.

Some of the people said, *What good is our Christ without hands?*

That gave someone else an idea, and he had a bronze plaque attached to the statue, engraved with these words: *I have no hands but your hands!*

One day a visitor saw it and was inspired to write a poem:

I have no hands but your hands, to do My work today.

I have no feet but your feet, to lead folks on the way.

I have no tongue but your tongue, to tell them how I died.

I have no help but your help, to bring them to God's side.

Christ Ministers Through People

The only way Christ can reach out His arms and lay His divine hands of blessing on lives, is through you. *You* are His Body now. His ministry in your community is expressed through *you* as a woman, the same as it is through any man.

He longs to speak to people about their salvation, and to convince them of the Gospel. Now He can do it through *you*. You are qualified as His witness.[Ac.1:8]

He wants to visit the lost, the sick and the prisoners and to bless them. Now He can do it through *you*. It is your mission as a woman, the same as it is for any man.

He will never send angels to do His work. He operates through you and me now. If you are too busy with other things or if you think you are not good enough, or if you feel that your own affairs are more important, or if you think you do not have time, then your Christ is like that statute; He has no hands.

And you may pray and fast for years, asking Him to visit your community, or for your nation or area to be evangelized, but it can only happen through *you!*

You Are God's Work Of Art

They say that Michelangelo started sculpturing at least 44 great statues in solid marble. But to our knowledge, he only finished 14 of them, such as the enormous statue of David in Florence, Italy, the Pieta in Rome's basilica, and his monumental Moses.

Just think: At least 30 great works of art were left unfinished. (Fortunately, the huge chunks of partially sculptured marble are preserved in an Italian museum.) Some show only a hand or a leg or an elbow and shoulder or a foot with toes. The total design in the great master artist's mind was never executed. The rest of the body remains frozen in solid marble, locked up forever, never to be formed into the great Michaelangelo's total design.

Could this be your case with God? The material in you is the best. You are redeemed — the full price has been paid. You are pure marble, so to speak.

And the Master Sculptor touched you with His miracle power, to make you a full, wonderful and perfect woman to reveal His power through. But for some reason you did not yield to His ideas. You did not grasp His viewpoint. You did not yield to full development. Only a part of you has ever been developed.

Tragedy Or Triumph

The greatest tragedy in life is for a woman or a man to live and die and to never realize the possibilities hidden within them.

The greatest triumph in life for a woman or a man is to discover yourself in Christ — to discover the rich, full happy life He created you for — then to allow Him to develop that unlimited life in you by sowing it in others and by reaping its results. That is *Life With Purpose.*

Now you have taken a new look at the great essentials in life which affect you as a woman of God.

FIRST: You have looked at *God* with a new vision. You have seen His *power,* His *love,* and that He is *present* here and now to meet you and to transform you.

SECOND: You have gotten His viewpoint of *others.* You have seen in them the true purpose of your own life and of expressing your own faith.

You have discovered the secret of the double-win in life: When you help others to win — *you* win. When you help others to succeed and grow — *you* succeed and grow. When you help others to find happiness — *you* discover happiness.

Blessings others is the secret of God's blessing on you, because what you give to others, others will give to you in good measure, pressed down, and shaken together, and running over.*Lu.6:38*

THIRD: You have gotten a new look at *yourself.* You have learned to see yourself as God sees you. You have learned to see yourself among the royal company of *Women And Self-Esteem.*

Time For Action

Now it is time to let the Lord know — by your action — that you embrace His attitude toward *Life With Purpose.*

What can you do? Confess what you believe; confess that His new dreams and ideas and concepts have become your new life-plan; then purpose to *do* something about them.

Paul covered the entire principle of conversion in two simple steps: 1) *If you believe in your heart that God raised Jesus from the dead,* and 2) *if you confess with your mouth that He is your Lord, you shall be saved.*Ro.10:9 That is the principle of receiving all blessings from God.

First: Believe it in your heart. That is your *faith.*

Second: Confess it with your mouth to others, share it with others, give it to others. That is your *ministry.*

This is one of the greatest moments of your life. You may be a young woman, and you want to be part of God's plan in life. You will never be the same again.

Older women can turn around too and begin a brand new positive useful life. It is never too late when you have had a fresh vision. David Ben Gurion learned French after he was seventy. The great painter, Titian, was painting masterpieces when he was ninety-eight years old.

Any woman or man is as young as their dreams, as their new projects, as their new ideals.

Almost 100 – Still On The Go

An old gentleman who was nearly one hundred years old came in a wheel chair to visit T.L. and me at our offices in Tulsa. He held meetings in the jail every week and won many souls to Christ.

He wanted a projector and our docu-miracle films. He was going to travel across America to show films and to tell people about Jesus. He was not a preacher, but he had God's idea about life.

He said, *I can't die! I can't die! I've got too much to do! Too many people are lost and need Jesus, and I've got to tell them!* He was nearly a hundred years old, but he did not have time to die. What a beautiful example of embracing God's attitude about *Life With Purpose* — and about people.

No one is too old and no one is too young. I was saved at the age of twelve. T.L. and I were married at ages seventeen and eighteen. We were missionaries in India at the ages of twenty and twenty-one. No one is too young. No one is too old. Today is *your* day.

New Commitment

I invite you to make a commitment to Jesus Christ. Let the Master Artist finish sculpting you until your finest potentials as a woman believer are discovered in full form.

See yourself as God sees you. See God's plans for you. See the unlimited possibilities that beckon you. You are part of a winning team. Nothing can stop you now.

Tell the Lord that you have decided to be part of His plan for others and to join His redeemed company of *Women and Self-Esteem*.

Prayer

Say this to God:

Oh, Lord — I have heard Your voice today. I believe that You have spoken to me. I want to be what You want me to be. I have seen a new vision today. New ideas have been planted in me as a woman of God.

You proved how much You loved me. You took my sins. Your blood was shed to make me clean.[Ro.5:8-9] **I believe on You, Lord.**

184

I receive Your new life. Thank You for the power that makes me a new creature.

The blood of Jesus Christ cleanses me.[1Jn.1:7] The life of Jesus Christ regenerates me.[1Pe.1:23] The joy of Jesus Christ fills me.[Jn.15:11Jn.16:24] I am of infinite value.[1Pe.1:7] Thank You that You love me. I am Yours.[Jn.6:37]

As a woman, redeemed by Your blood, you have made my body Your temple. I am accepted. I am commissioned in Your Kingdom.[1Co.6:19-20] I am part of Your family.

I am as valuable to You as anyone. I have Your nature. I am loved. I can love others. Whatever I sow in others, I will reap.[Ga.6:8]

I will feed the hungry. I will give drink to the thirsty. I will clothe the naked. I will visit the sick and the prisoners.

As a woman-follower of Christ, I realize that I can only serve You as I serve others. I can only love You as I love others. Thank You that I am part of Your plan. I have a place that no one else can fill.[Ep.2:10]

No longer will I make negative confessions about myself or about my womanhood. No longer will I condemn myself. No longer will I destroy what You value.[Ac.10:15]

I now realize that, as a woman I am accepted. I can do Your work. I am born again. I am a new creature. I have repented of my old traditions. I have changed my mind about myself.

I see YOU — Oh, Lord — with new eyes. I see OTHERS — as You see them. I see MYSELF — in Your image.

Together we cannot fail. Father, everything is possible for You.*Mk.10:36a AB* Thank You. Lord! In Jesus' Name!

Amen!

VI

PARTNERSHIP
WITH
GOD

SOME PEOPLE BELIEVE that the prosperous woman is proud, greedy and self-centered, but that the woman without financial means is humble, generous and charitable.

Because of this traditional propensity, millions of Christian women fail to develop their innate talents and abilities, living out their lives in resigned subordination, usually without the thought of material accomplishment or of creative productivity.

It is not logical for a woman's academic and business potential to be wasted in the monotonous, noncreative world of pushbuttons and soap operas.

This outdated ideal for a woman gradually stifles her creativity as she surrenders to the self-image of perennial servitude and of dependent submission. Such a surrender neutralizes much of her inherent skill and resourcefulness.

Partnership With God is for women the same as it is for men, but they must apply themselves in creative thinking, in enterprise and in industry in a competitive world, as all successful people must do.

As a woman believer, decide to be a finance-partner with God, in lifting and in blessing hurting and despairing people.

Chapter 6

PARTNERSHIP WITH GOD

DOES GOD WILL material prosperity for the Christian woman? Or is it God's plan for the daughters of His family to be dependent upon men for their material needs in order to keep them humble, submissive and subservient?

The fact is that the Bible abounds with clear-cut promises of prosperity and of material abundance for women the same as for men, when they regard money positively - as a means for accomplishing God's purpose on earth.

Abilities For Facilities

There is a traditional concept, particularly in the religions and cultures of the modern industrialized world, that a woman's place is in the home; that God never endowed her with the intellectual capacity for achievement in business or with the faculties for success in enterprise.

It is somewhat of a paradox to this *Westernized*

notion, that throughout most of the so-called Third World, women are often the real entrepreneurs, respected for their innate business and marketing ingenuity.

Yet, in the modernized world, religion and culture combine to foster an irrational ideal for women. Although she is expected to be educated and academically competent, as soon as she is married, it is assumed that she will accept passively her assigned role in life and graciously adopt a subordinate, submissive and subservient function.

After accepting a man in her life, it is often assumed that the woman will affably relinquish whatever career, vocation or profession she had aspired to or was involved in, abdicating her scholastic qualifications in favor of becoming a good and proper *housewife.* Often, this means being a general unpaid maid and servant to the man she has married.

This image persists, despite modern technology which has rendered it impractical and inappropriate in today's hi-tech household.

Because of this traditional propensity, millions of Christian women fail to develop their innate talents and abilities, living out their lives in resigned subordination, usually without the thought of material accomplishment or of creative productivity.

Mama — A *Bona Fide* Homemaker

I was born in Merced, California, one of eleven children, raised near there. We eked out a meager subsistence, farming the ground and working in the orchards.

Being the tenth child, I cut my teeth in life watching my mother toil day and night as the *homemaker.*

All the water for household needs had to be pumped from the old well. Then it was carried in buckets to our rough wood floor kitchen. Mama built and stoked the fire to heat it in a big iron kettle for washing. She spent hours of back-breaking drudgery over the galvanized washtub and scrub board, toiling to keep the family's home-made clothes and scanty bedding clean.

Mama sewed all of our clothes, hand-knitted all of our sweaters, socks and *woolens,* grew the vegetables, cooked every meal over a wood stove, churned the butter, scrubbed the floors on her knees, canned the fruit, hand-quilted our bedding, baked our bread, *etc.*

That is a *bona fide homemaker.* No wonder the family's survival depended on her expertise.

But by what twist of human logic does religion and culture insist that the modern wife, with a hi-tech equipped house, conform to the image of my mama.

In the typical modern house, how much time and

how much energy are really necessary to be a home-maker?

Today's modern housewife and househusband have the advantages of quick-pack, well balanced, frozen dinners and microwave ovens, sealed or canned foods, drinks and quick-serve desserts; push-button dishwashers, garbage disposals, washers, dryers, vacuum cleaners, running hot and cold water, paper dishes, plastic dinnerware, disposable diapers, ready-made clothing, electric blankets, and so much more — all valued time and energy savers.

Women And Foremothers

It is not logical for a woman's academic and business potential to be wasted in the monotonous, non-creative world of pushbuttons and soap operas.

To restrict God's woman today to a role which befit her foremothers, would be like the religious dictums which limit men to the mechanisms of the horse-and-buggy era because they befit the image of their forefathers.

The Snare Of Traditional Dependency

This outdated ideal for a woman gradually stifles her creativity as she surrenders to the self-image of perennial servitude and of dependent submission. Such a surrender neutralizes much of her inherent skill and resourcefulness.

By the time a woman's children are in school, if she has not chosen to, or been allowed to exercise her innate or acquired expertise and her skill potential, she may unwittingly lose her drive for accomplishment, and actually come to prefer the comforts of her traditional dependency.

When that happens, something precious and vital dies in the woman. The man in her life has usually done the vital thinking and has made the principal decisions concerning her life. The creative strategy for survival or for growth has been up to him. Consequently the woman has likely never sensed the satisfaction of material productivity nor the self-esteem of achievement.

Often, women who are divorced or widowed, find themselves unexercised in strategic planning or in an enterprise, incompetent in business, inexperienced in the workplace, unqualified for employment and unaccustomed to the simplest requirements for life. Many women have never experienced the simple dignity of having a personal bank account, of owning a piece of property in their name, of signing a business contract. Many of them have never written a check or have never made the most ordinary business decision.

Nothing Is Impossible
For God And A Woman

Partnership With God is for women the same as it is

for men, but they must apply themselves in creative thinking, in enterprise and in industry in a competitive world, as all successful people must do.

I have written this book to encourage you, as a woman, to discover your own dignity and your own destiny in God's plan, as His friend and as His partner in doing His work. Allow your indigenous talents and abilities to come to life. Become alert to your own potential. Reach out and become a learner. Up-grade your own attitude. Learn to see yourself in *Partnership With God*, doing His wonderful Kingdom business of blessing, lifting, healing and saving human persons as a *Woman With Self-Esteem.*

Decide that God is depending on you, as a woman, to accomplish His work. Believe for Him to impart His wisdom to you. There is nothing impossible for God and a woman.

To experience the fulfillment of *Partnership With God*, accept His promises, claim them and ACT on them — exactly like an unsaved person who claims forgiveness or like a sick person who claims healing by faith.

You will do that when you, as a woman, decide to liberate yourself from the restricted female image of the past, and apply yourself as a capable, positive, creative producer in your world.

The Perfect Partnership

As a woman believer, are YOU willing to be a finance-partner with God, in lifting and in blessing hurting and despairing people?

Is your attitude: *My place, as a woman, is to concede in life and to fill whatever role others expect of me?*

Or is it: *As a woman, I choose to identify with God in His love plan for people. I understand that money can be a sacred tool for soulwinning. I will be God's partner to reach hurting human persons and to bless them!*

Giving to reach souls, is a ministry. A Christian woman's money represents her life.

When she invests it to reach the UNreached, she is as much a minister or a missionary as the one who goes to the frontlines, or who announces the good news to the people. But unless she decides to become active in some wage-earning or money-producing enterprise in her own name, how can she become an effective finance-partner with God and discover the exhilaration and the self-esteem of accomplishments with Him.

Why Poverty?

When God created the first woman and man, He placed them in a world of material plenty. He commanded the waters and the ground to *bring forth ABUNDANTLY.*[Ge.1:20] *God blessed them, saying BE*

195

FRUITFUL AND MULTIPLY.[Ge.1:21-22] Then He placed Adam and Eve in control of this abundance.

But Satan's intervention in God's love plan enticed the woman and the man to sin against God, which resulted in their separation from Him.[Is.59:2]

God said to them: *Cursed is the ground for your sake; in sorrow shall you eat of it all the days of your life; thorns also and thistles shall it bring forth to you; ... in the sweat of your face shall you eat bread, until you return to the ground.*[Ge.3:17-19]

Now you can understand the reason for human destitution and material lack — and why God planned *Partnership With God* for women (as well as for men).

Not Born For Slavery

The economic problems which exasperate and harass women are the issue of the deeper problem of estrangement from God's principles for life.

Every way you turn there are demands placed upon you with which you cannot cope. Food, clothing and shelter — the bare necessities of life are secured only by constant struggle.

In the midst of a world of God's abundance, you toil, you borrow, you mortgage — and in spite of all you can do, there is often not enough to make ends meet at your house. This is the devil's strategy to break your will and to reduce you to the level of slavery.

God never created women for such a struggle in life. When God created Eve, He placed her, with her man, in the most beautiful garden of abundant living. There was total prosperity for Eve, the same as for Adam. It was what God designed every woman to live in. It was His dream of contentment, of harmony, of abundance.

Then the master deceiver paid them a visit and they yielded to his subtle temptation to question what God had said.[Ge.3:1] Through their *lust of the flesh* and their *pride of life,*[1Jn.2:16] they partook of the forbidden fruit,[Ge.3:6] transgressing God's law, thereby forfeiting the garden of blessing which God had given to them.[Ge.3:23-24]

Greed, jealousy, lust and deceit produced the evils of human society where the strong dominated the weak, where the rich ruled over the poor, where men subjugated the women, where lords became masters over peasants — all of which was the result of sin.

Pleasure gave way to anguish. Happiness and love turned to discontentment and lust. Health became poisoned by disease. Abundance degenerated into want, destitution and depravity. God's dream for people was aborted.

God Is Spirit!
You As A Woman, Are His Flesh!

Jesus explained it all when He said:

The thief (Satan) *comes only to STEAL, and to KILL, and to DESTROY.*[Jn.10:10]

But God *is not willing that ANY should perish, but that ALL should come to repentance.*[2Pe.3:9]

You, as a woman, were not born to be a slave, but to be an *heir of God — a joint-heir with Jesus Christ*[Ro.8:16-17; Ga.3:29] — to be God's friend and partner.

You see, God is Spirit! You, as a woman, are His flesh! Whatever He does, He does it through His body — the church, which is people — ordinary women and men like you and me.

Woman's Priority

God's No. 1 priority is to share the gospel with every creature, in all the world.[Mk.16:15] The highest priority a Jesus-woman can have is to be part of God's No. 1 plan. To do that, a Christian woman must learn about God's prosperity-plan for herself, and she must appropriate His plan for material blessing in her own life.

When I was just a little girl, I learned from my mother and father how to take the tiny seeds and sow them in the rich farm soil. I marveled at how much God gave us in return for the small amount which we gave to the earth.

Jesus taught that every promise He gave was a seed. He said, *the seed is the word of God.*[Lu.8:11] That seed of His promise is *incorruptible*[1Pe.1:23] (undecaying, immortal, imperishable). The life in each seed of God's promise cannot die, or decay, or perish. — God's seed promises cannot fail.

Christ said: *The words that I speak to you are Spirit and they are life.*[Jn.6:63]

There is life in each seed. That life is from God — the author of life.

Every time good seed is sown in good soil, the sower reaps an increased return. This law is as irrefutable as the law of gravity.

It is impossible for a woman to plant one kernel of corn and to reap only one kernel.

God wants women to see that *It is He who gives them power to get wealth.*[De.8:18] *Riches and wealth are the gift of God.*[Ec.5:19]

God wants women to see that giving and receiving money is a flowing interchange between their act of faith and His unlimited supply. It is based on His infallible law of sowing and reaping.

A Woman-Partner With God

A farmer sets aside the choice grain (the *Firstfruits*) and gives it back to mother earth. In return, the earth gives back an abundance of the same kind of seed that was sown, and that farmer's *barns are filled with PLENTY.*[Pr.3:9-10] That way, the farmer has more to sow — on greater fields.

God's program of reaching lost souls with the gospel requires enormous sums of money. He wants every woman believer to learn the secret of financial prosperity. Bring your money and sow it as seed-money in the fertile soil of soulwinning, and let God prove that your seed-money will give you back a return of more than you gave.

Blessed is the one who fears the Lord, who delights in His commandments. WEALTH AND RICHES shall be in your house. [Ps.112:1,3] *The Lord has pleasure in the PROSPERITY of His servant.*[Ps.35:27]

See yourself as a woman-partner with God — His finance-partner, one in whose care He can entrust His wealth in a flowing interchange of giving and receiving. Then expect God's miracle return, *pressed down, shaken together, running over.*[Lu.6:38] He will do it if He must perform a material miracle to do it.

A Woman And Miracles

God performed a material miracle to provide money for the disciples to pay their taxes.[Mt.17:27]

He performed a material miracle to provide bread and meat and water for the Israelites in the wilderness.[Ex.16:14-17] He even miraculously prevented their shoes from wearing out.^{De.29:5}

God performed a material miracle for a widow whose creditors were coming to take her sons as bond-servants. Miraculously she poured enough oil from a single cruse to fill many vessels full, which she sold for money to pay off her creditors. It was a miracle.^{2K.4:1-7}

Jesus Christ performed a material miracle to supply food for 5,000 hungry people in the desert.^{Mt.14: 14-21}

The question is: Will God perform a material miracle to supply your needs?

Will God still save an unconverted woman? Yes — if she knows God's covenant, believes His promises and acts upon them with her faith.

Will God still heal a sick woman? Yes — if the sick woman knows God's covenant of healing, believes His promises and acts upon them with her faith.

Will God still multiply the finances or miraculously increase the possessions of a woman? Yes — if she knows God's covenant of prosperity and acts upon His promises with her faith.

Scriptures For Women

I've always marveled at the way some women believe strongly that the Bible verses promising salvation are for women, as well as for men. But they have never claimed the multitude of promises about their *Partnership With God.*

Women believers do not hesitate to claim: *Whoever shall call on the name of the Lord shall be saved.*[Ro.10:13] *You shall receive power after that the Holy Spirit is come upon you.*[Ac.1:8] *This same Jesus shall so come in like manner as you have seen Him go.*[Ac.1:11]

But few Christian women ever claim verses like those included in this book. As you read them, ask yourself: *Do I truly BELIEVE these Bible verses are for me as a woman?*

Let me cite this scripture like this:

Beloved daughter of mine, I wish ABOVE ALL THINGS, that you may PROSPER and be in health, even as your soul prospers.[3Jn.1:2]

Prosper in that verse means *to succeed, thrive, be successful; to be safe in mind, body and material estate; to have peace and a secure welfare; to be secure and wealthy.* That describes God's desire for you as a woman.

God WILLS *above all things* that you PROSPER in three ways: in *finances*, in *health*, in a *full life*.

But Jesus said, *You make the word of God of none effect by your tradition,*[Mt.15:6] which is *an inherited culture, attitude or belief.* These words *of none effect* actually mean *to cancel or to void God's promises by contrary beliefs or traditions.* Webster says this means *to reduce to nothing — to make void — to render of no legal value — to destroy the force of.*

As a woman, you can *reduce God's word to nothing* or *render it of no legal value* or *destroy its force* or *annul and invalidate it by your tradition.*$^{Mt.15:6}$ That is what you do to His promises about prosperity if you cling to the belief that God wants you, as a woman, to be subordinated in life without personal means, without material achievements, without the self-pride of personal enterprise and without the self-esteem and the dignity of realizing personal success.

The *traditional* belief that prosperity for women is wrong, or that it is not for you, nullifies God's plan for your material blessings.

But when you read God's promises and act on them, God will fulfill them in your life — even if He must perform material miracles to do it, like miraculously multiplying the widow's oil and meal, or the lad's lunch that fed 5,000.

Women Witnesses

I could fill pages with testimonies of women who have learned to give by faith in God's word, then who have experienced His miraculous return. When they began, they were wage earners. Today they are owners of businesses. When they began, they were renters. Today they are property owners.

Our mail brings a constant stream of testimonies from Christian women who have put God's word to the test and who have experienced His prosperity in return. That is a big step for *Women And Self-Esteem.*

The Lord shall make you plenteous in goods, in the fruit of your cattle, and in the fruit of your ground.^{De.28:11} That applies to you as a woman.

Plenteous in that verse means *to exceed, to excel, to abound, to profit, to be abundant.* It means *yielding abundantly more than sufficient; a great or rich supply; generous sufficiency; large supply; copious yield.*

In other words, the Bible says: *The Lord will make you abundant and generous in goods; He will give you a great and rich supply.*

The Lord will command His blessing on your storehouses, and in all that you set your hand to do.^{De.28:8}

Blessed shall be the fruit of your ground and the fruit of your cattle, the increase of your cattle and the flocks of your sheep.^{De.28:4}

Blessed shall be your basket and your store.^{De.28:5}

These are promises made to every woman, *if you will hearken to the voice of the Lord and observe His commandments.*^{De.28:1}

God's will is *that you, always having all sufficiency in all things, may abound in every good work.*^{2Co.9:8} God wills that you be *enriched in everything to all bountifulness.*^{2Co.9:11} He wills your *liberal distribution ... to all people.*^{2Co.9:13} To do this, God wills your prosperity and He has provided abundant promises to back up

His will.

*It is He who gives you power to get wealth,*De.8:18 and it is He who set in order His principle of sowing and reaping for women as well as for men.

Miracle Of Dollar Bills

I remember a time of dire financial need when my husband, T.L. Osborn, and I were young. I did not have a coat. It was rainy, fall weather in California. We were riding buses to preach the gospel.

We attended a conference where the urgent need for a large missionary press was presented. Before that conference ended, we borrowed a hundred dollars and planted it as seed-money in the Lord's work, to help buy that press.

Very soon we were reaping an abundant return from that seed-gift. A woman bought me a beautiful new coat. A man presented us the title to an automobile. Money came from unexpected sources. God's law could not fail.

Another time, our faith was tested. We had purchased a car and we planned to pay for it through monthly installments. But that particular month we had given everything we had received. Whenever we saw an opportunity to win more souls, we planted our seed-money. We believed that the more we planted, the larger return we could claim. Our needs were large, so we planted liberally.

Our car payment was due. We lacked fourteen dollars. We had sown our seed-money, so we were believing for God's abundant return. We prayed earnestly for God to meet our need. We knew the seed-dollars which we had sown must produce an increased return — even if God had to perform a material miracle. We were proving God — putting Him to the test as He said to do.[Mal.3:10]

That night, we locked the doors of our small room and went to bed. No one knew our needs but God alone. What happened will sound ridiculous and incredible, in the natural, but it is true. God performed a material miracle to prove His promises in our lives.

When we awoke, one-dollar bills were strewn all over that room, as though they had literally been dropped from heaven, fluttering down onto the bed, the floor, behind the table, under the divan, *etc.* We gathered up the dollar bills as reverently as the children of Israel gathered the manna from heaven,[Ex.16:17-18] or as the disciples gathered the fragments of bread which Christ had multiplied.[Jn.6:12-13]

We looked in every nook and cranny of that room, and when we had gathered the last bill we could find, we counted them and there were thirteen one-dollar bills.

Knowing God had done a miracle, we believed there must be one more dollar bill which we had missed. Finally, we lifted the old icebox away from the wall, and there was the fourteenth dollar bill, exactly the amount we needed to meet our obligation on time!

We had sown dollars, now we were reaping them. And before that month ended, our harvest was abundantly more than we had sown.

Planting To Reap

When Elijah visited the widow in Zarephath during the famine, she was destitute, preparing to cook her last cake of meal, then she and her son planned to die.

Elijah directed her to bake him a cake first! This seemed cruel and heartless. But when she obeyed, it was like a farmer planting the choice seed. That last cake became her seed-cake. It produced a bountiful return — a harvest of much more than she gave to Elijah. *Her barrel wasted not nor did her cruse of oil fail.*1K.17:9-16

One of the greatest hindrances to women for *Partnership With God* is the tradition inherited by them. I have heard them say: *Oh, I give because I want to. As a woman, I don't expect anything in return.*

Suppose a widow, left with a farm, said: *I sow these fields each spring because I love to plant seed, but I expect no harvest.* How long could she survive?

A good woman farmer expects a good harvest. Good seed always produces a good return for women as much as for men.

Three Facts About Planting

Each time you set aside your FIRSTfruits or a seed-gift to plant in the Lord's work, remember these three fundamental facts about *Partnership With God.*

FIRST: As a woman believer, keep your expectations only on the Lord. He alone is your supply — your only source! God shall supply all of your needs.[Ph.4:19] HE is the life of every good seed. HE is the creator of all wealth. HE is the source from which your abundant return must flow.

When you plant your seed-money and anticipate your increased harvest, do not limit your increase to your employer's willingness to raise your salary, or to an increased interest or dividend on your savings or securities, or to an enlarged paycheck, annuity, a better job, *etc?*

GOD is the source of your supply. He may use those means, but He is not limited to them! Keep your eyes on HIM — not on the means He might use. HE, and He alone is the source of your expectations.

SECOND: When you, as a woman, plant your seed-money in the Lord's work, remember to plant with an increased return in mind. In other words, plant objectively!

Your giving must be productive. Jesus said, *It is*

more blessed (productive) *to give than to receive.*^{Ac.20:35} If your giving does not produce a return of more than you give, how will evangelism be financed to-morrow? *Ac.20:35*

Every time you invest in God's work of reaching lost souls, you are planting seed-money so that you may reap more than you give — so that you may sow more the next time and then reap a greater return for the Lord's work.

This is Christian stewardship!

This is *Partnership With God!*

This takes vision and demands faith. This calls for action and believing. This is why tradition has developed the easier way of keeping and losing — and of dying.

THIRD: When you, as a woman, sow your seed-money in God's work, expect an increased return! Expect a miracle! Expect more back than you gave! Expect God to fulfill His promise! Expect a financial harvest! Expect divine intervention to return to you more than you gave. Expect God to make His word good to you — a woman believer.

Without faith it is impossible to please Him; for anyone who comes to God must believe that He is a rewarder. Mk.9:23; He.11:6

There can be no miracle without expectation. After you have sown your seed-money, expect growth.

And keep your expectation on God as your only source because, as Paul said, *God gives the increase.*[1Co.3:6] Once you have acted in faith on His word of promise, you have every right to expect a miracle return. Once you have sown, expect to reap! Without expectation, faith is dead!

Christ gave the Great Commission, then He chose you and me to carry it out. That requires enormous sums of money.

That is why God wills partnership with Him for *Women With Self-Esteem* who choose to be part of His plan to bless humanity.

Women And Partnership With God

That is why *He has given to us exceeding great and precious promises.*[2Pe.1:4]

Now *those who seek the Lord LACK NO GOOD THING.*[Ps.34:10]

My God shall supply ALL YOUR NEED.[Ph.4:19]

The Lord will open to you HIS GOOD TREASURE. [De.28:12]

The blessing of the Lord BRINGS WEALTH.[Pr.10:22 NIV]

The Lord shall command the BLESSING UPON YOU ... in all that you set your hand to.[De.28:8]

The condition is to *only believe*[He.11:6] the gospel message that Christ redeemed you, as a woman, from your sins and from their effects.[Ga.3:13] He attributed all of your sins to His account and He paid for them. He did that so that He could credit all of His righteousness to your account.[2Co.5:21 LB]

God took the sinless Christ and poured into Him your sins. Then, in exchange, He poured God's goodness into you.[2Co.5:21 LB]

Now that God did that for you, from the moment that you believe it and accept it, the righteousness of Jesus Christ is credited to your account.

That is the key to *Partnership With God.*

Power To Prosper

It is God's will that every woman be reborn to the abundant life. From the moment you accept Jesus Christ by faith, you become a royal daughter in God's Family, with all of the legal and equal rights of any family member. Realizing that produces a *Rebirth Of Self-Worth* in you and it puts you among God's *Women With Self-Esteem.*

God wants you to enjoy His best!

Prosperity Promises

He challenges you to bring of whatever money you have to Him, and to *PROVE HIM with it NOW ... and see if He will not open you the windows of heaven, and pour you out a blessing, that there shall not be room enough to receive.*[Mal.3:10]

For the Lord God says ... your barrel of meal shall not waste, neither shall your cruse of oil fail.[1K.17:14]

For the earth is the Lord's and the FULLNESS thereof.[1Co.10:26]

You shall make your way PROSPEROUS, and you shall have GOOD SUCCESS.[Jos.1:8]

Seek first the expansion of God's Kingdom worldwide, and ALL THESE THINGS SHALL BE ADDED UNTO YOU.[Mt.6:33 RV]

The Lord is your shepherd, YOU SHALL NOT WANT.[Ps.23:1]

NO GOOD THING will He withhold from them that walk uprightly.[Ps.84:11]

Blessed are you when you fear the Lord, when you delight greatly in His commandments. WEALTH AND RICHES shall be in your house.[Ps.112:1,3]

The silver is mine, and the gold is mine.[Hag.2:8] *All the earth is mine.*[Ex.19:5] *The land is mine.*[Le.25:23] *Every beast of the forest is mine, and the cattle on a thousand hills.*[Ps.50:10] *How excellent is your lovingkindness, O God! therefore ... people put their trust under ... your wings. They shall be ABUNDANTLY SATISFIED ... for with you is THE FOUNTAIN (source) of LIFE.*[Ps.36:7-9]

O Lord, how MANIFOLD are your works ... the earth is FULL OF YOUR RICHES ... you open your hands, they are FILLED WITH GOOD.[Ps.104:24,28]

Those who seek Me early shall find Me. RICHES AND HONOR are with Me; yes, durable RICHES and righteousness ... that I may cause those who love Me to INHERIT SUBSTANCE. and I will FILL THEIR TREASURES. Pr.8:17-18,21

Blessed are you, Lord God ... FOR ALL THAT IS IN THE HEAVEN AND IN THE EARTH IS YOURS ... Both RICHES and HONOR come from you. 1Ch.29:10-12

Walk in God's ways ... that YOU MAY PROSPER IN ALL THAT YOU DO and wherever you turn yourself. 1K.2:3

Blessed is the Lord, who DAILY LOADS YOU WITH BENEFITS. Ps.68:19

A faithful person shall ABOUND WITH BLESSINGS. Pr.28:20

Keep ... the words of this covenant ... that you may PROSPER IN ALL THAT YOU DO. De.29:9

I am come that you may have LIFE, and that you may have it MORE ABUNDANTLY. Jn.10:10

The world of ABUNDANCE that God has created all around you is proof that He wills that women live in material *Partnership With God* the same as men do.

There is no (woman) who has left house, or brothers, or sisters, or father, or mother, or (husband), or children, or lands, for My sake, and the gospel's, but (she) shall receive A HUNDREDFOLD NOW IN THIS TIME,

HOUSES AND LOVED ONES AND LANDS ... and in the world to come eternal life.[Mk.10:29-30]

Partnership With God is His will for every woman (the same as it is for men), so that they may bring part of their money and dedicate it to send the gospel *to every creature.* When you do this, you become a co-worker or a partner with God — a missionary or preacher just as much as the one who goes abroad. And you not only receive a *missionary's* reward; but God miraculously returns your money ... *good measure, pressed down, running over.*[Lu.6:38] It is His covenant. He cannot break it.

Always remember: God's prosperity is for *YOU* as a woman, the same as it is for any man, and today, number yourself among God's royal personae of *Women And Self-Esteem.*

You are marked by destiny. God has already planned your future. He trusts in your cooperation to fulfill His love plan for people. He believes in you. He wants to prosper and to bless you. Then you can be a blessing to others. That is why this powerful book has come into your hands.

May God richly bless you.

VII

IF I
WERE A
WOMAN

IF I WERE A WOMAN, I would embrace total salvation and never acquiesce before any doctrine, teaching or cultural tradition which impugns me or denies my worthiness as Christ's witness, His representative, His ambassador or His co-worker in any private or public ministry to which He leads or inspires or calls me

Are class and sex discriminations of archaic Bible cultures to be imposed today? Only upon women? Are women redeemed, but kept at a distance? Restored, but unworthy to speak for Christ who justified them? Are their sins forgiven, but held against them, while the sins of *man*kind are expunged forever?

No royal daughter of God's family should allow religious dogmas to confine her in subservience, submission, subjection or subordination.

Can believing women afford to bow to discrimination in the church world, while in the secular world their equality is a fact of life?

Should a woman who believes in redemption, and who desires to share the good news, allow men or systems to forbid her from doing what Jesus commissioned her to do?

If I were a woman, I would not surrender to the repression of my ministry. If someone told me that I could not publicly teach or preach about Jesus, I would thank God for my voice and for my right of choice to obey my Lord as His anointed witness and authorized representative.

Chapter 7

IF I WERE A WOMAN

By T.L. Osborn
(Enlarged Edition)

PART 1

INTRODUCTION

WHEN WOMEN UNDERSTAND their total salvation and recognize their own equality in God's plan, they usually become involved in some kind of personal or public ministry to needy people. Discovering their individual dignity and their destiny in God's redemptive plan emancipates them forever from the primitive bias of sex discrimination which has so impeded women in Christian ministry.

Chauvinistic manipulation of womankind has permeated the religions of the world for many long centuries. The influence of medieval cultures and of archaic dogmas still dictates stubborn suppression of women in the church.

But contrary to religious female subjugation,

217

the message of the gospel — Christ's message of good news is that, when redemption was accomplished, women the same as men were justified and restored to God as though no sin had ever been committed.

To continue the doctrine of female inferiority and of her ineligibility for certain ministries in which only men are worthy to serve, is to mitigate the redemptive work of Christ on a sexual basis.

The redemption of humankind through Christ's vicarious death, burial and resurrection restored both women and men to God. To argue that womankind is forever disqualified for public ministry and suited only for subservient roles, while exonerating mankind from all effects of sin, is to limit Christ's redemptive work for women, while embracing its total effect for men. This is interpreting the redemptive sacrifice of Christ on a sexual basis.

Redemption, therefore, being a fact, if I were a woman, I would no longer permit outdated traditions from medieval societies to incriminate me as a royal daughter in God's family, nor to restrain me from my highest possible achievement and fulfillment in whatever level of private or public ministry God put in my heart to exercise.

I will pour out My Spirit on all flesh; your sons and your daughters shall prophesy ...

And also on My menservants and on My maid-servants I will pour out My Spirit in those days ... Whoever calls on the name of the Lord shall be saved.[Jl.2:28-32]

If I were a woman with a desire to obey Christ and to be His witness [Ac.1:8] in whatever capacity I felt He inspired or called or led me, I would accept Joel's prophecy as being for me; I would act upon Christ's words and allow Him to speak and to minister through me to the fullest extent by which He could use me

If I were a woman I would not permit myself, or my status, or my ministry as a woman to be demeaned or depreciated to a subservient level by the traditions and dictums of male clergymen.

* * *

PART 2

WHEN WOMEN PROPHESY

THE VITAL ISSUE of women in public ministry has been stubbornly resisted by most Christian institutions. Traditional pentecostals and charismatics generally pretend that they have no problem with the issue.

It is vital that women believers be encouraged in whatever Christian ministry they may feel called or impressed by their Lord to exercise. To do this, there are two aspects of Joel's inspired words about *daughters* and about *handmaidens* prophesying *in the last days,* (Ac. 2:14-18) which merit more careful attention than they have had in the past.

When the women were assembled with the men at the first outpouring of the Holy Spirit (Acts 1:14; 2:1-4, 14-18), Peter quoted Joel's prophecy: *Your daughters shall PROPHESY* — and *handmaidens ... shall PROPHESY* a double emphasis of the public ministry of women after the Holy Spirit was given to the followers of Christ.

Traditional and historic churches generally ignore these statements and continue to deny *women* and *handmaidens* any public ministerial authority or endorsement.

Charismatic and Pentecostal bodies generally assume that they sanction such ministries by women, but they maintain a sort of unwritten code of approved activities or of ministerial guidelines which carefully circumscribes a woman's range of ministerial expression. This unwritten code is kept in force largely because of contemporary *submission* teaching, but also because of the limiting prevalent interpretation of what the word, *prophesy* means

One of the most highly esteemed reference sources, among both Jewish and Christian scholars of Biblical language, is the monumental, 10 volume *Theological Dictionary of the New Testament, edited by G. Kittel* and published by Eerdmans (over ten thousand pages).

What *Prophesy* Means

Volume VI of the Kittel Dictionary series, devotes 80 pages to the meaning of the word *Prophesy.*

On page 783, the first linguistic aspect of the word is: *to speak, to declare openly, to make known publicly;* footnote 4: *to proclaim publicly in the people's assembly, aloud, as an oracle* (of God) — and an *oracle* means: *a medium by which God reveals knowledge and makes known His divine purpose ... the revelation or utterance issued from divinity through a priest or priestess ...* and it clearly includes Christian teaching (He. 5:12, 1Pe. 4:11).

Volume VI of Kittel's dictionary collection continues, on page 848, to define *primitive Christian PROPHECY* (as) *the inspired speech of charismatic preachers through whom are made known God's plan of salvation for the world and the community of His will for the life of Christians,* (including) *divine mysteries* (and) *God's saving will for the Gentiles* (all people; also) *admonishing the indolent and weary* (and) *encouraging those under assault, speaking with a sense of God-given authority, giving authoritative instruction ...*

All of this (and there are 80 pages of definition) makes it very clear that the ministry of *daughters* and of *handmaidens prophesying,* is an unlimited, all inclusive exercise of private and of public ministry in the church and in the world — no different and no more restricted than it is for *sons* and for *servants* of God.

Medieval Restraints

The traditional restraints impeding women from public ministry result from two brief statements made by Paul. (1Co. 14:34 and 1Ti. 2:12) One proof that Paul did not intend to silence women in general, is clearly indicated by his statement in 1Co. 11:5: *Every woman who prays or prophesies* ... She could not do this if she remained silent.

GOD'S WOMAN

by T.L. Osborn

God's woman,
    She has been redeemed;
God's woman,
    She has new esteem.

    She's come alive,
    She's on the rise,
    She has a choice.
    She has a voice.

God's Woman,
    With a mission and a call;
God's Woman,
    With a vision for us all.

    She's anointed. She's a witness.
    She's appointed. She is gifted.
    Christ is her identity
    Of dignity and destiny.

The blood of Christ removed her shame.
    Now she acts in Jesus' name.
The power of the Holy Ghost,
    Has sent her to the uttermost.

God's Woman,
    Of faith and hope and power
God's Woman,
    With life and love this hour.

Any time that my wife, Dr. Daisy, is reminded of Paul's words for *women to be silent in the church,* she reminds herself that Paul also counseled *EVERY woman who ... PROPHESIES.* His advice for women to be silent clearly had to do with a local, societal problem. To apply that advice to all women, universally, would contradict the many admonishments of Christ and the examples of so many active women ministers in the Early Church.

When women function in both private and public ministries, under the anointing and direction of the Holy Spirit, they fulfill the words of the prophets, the unchanging plan of God, the teachings of Jesus Christ and the ministry of believers as Christ's witnesses, co-laborers and ambassadors. Jesus authorized the women, as well as the men, to be His *witnesses* (Acts 1:8, 14), and approved of them both, *to the uttermost part of the earth*

And we should not forget that this divine sanction by Christ was given to women who, in their own culture and religion, were forbidden as legal *witnesses* in any court of law. Yet Jesus told them, in essence: *You qualify to be MY WITNESSES. You count in My Kingdom. You shall be witnesses for Me ... unto the uttermost parts of the earth.*

Prophecy Unlimited

Kittel's dictionary says further, on page 854, that "prophecy" *is not addressed solely to Christians; it also has missionary significance.* (The preaching of prophets or prophetesses) *lead non-Christians to recognition of their guilt and to worship God.* Page 855: *The Prophet is the Spirit-endowed counsellor of the community who tells it what to do in specific situations ..., whose preaching contains admonition and comfort and calls for repentance* (and gives God's) *promises.*

All of this propounds unlimited ministries for *daughters and for handmaidens* of the Lord, *in the last days, who PROPHESY.* God's authorized scope of ministry for women is infinitely broader than what has been neatly circumscribed for them by the contemporary charismatocracy.

The purpose of this book is to increase every woman believer's understanding of her potential field of ministry, and in that way, increase the distinguished ranks of God's anointed *Women And Self-Esteem.*

* * *

PART 3

PROPHECY FULFILLMENT ASSUMED OR PROPHECY IN ACTION

THERE IS A SECOND aspect of Joel's words about *daughters* and *handmaidens* in prophesying ministries, which needs more careful attention. It is the popular but mistaken concept that *what is prophetically re-*

corded in Holy Writ will, in some divine way and at some appointed time, just come to pass — whether believers do anything about it or not.

The prevalent Christian *mind-set* overlooks the eminent fact that prophecy is fulfilled *through people,* and *by people.*

Traditional Christian leaders usually make the mistake of *assuming the fulfillment of prophecy* — especially those portions about which they have little or no interest, such as matters concerning women. They piously quote Joel's words: *It shall come to pass in the last days, saith God, that I will pour out of My Spirit upon ALL flesh; and your sons and your DAUGHTERS shall prophesy* ... Jl. 2:28; Ac. 2:17.

How do theologians expect this to happen, and when? And in what way do anti-women-in-public-ministry camps plan to accommodate this fulfillment of prophecy? Do they actually plan to accept and to honor the prophesying ministries of these *daughters?* At what point in time? How do they expect it to happen? Will female angelic beings appear supernaturally on their platforms, *prophesying* to their assemblage? Would this be tolerated by conventional authority? How are Joel's words to be fulfilled.

How Prophecy Is Fulfilled

Prophecy cannot be *presumed* to be fulfilled.

Prophecy is the divine utterance of events which

God wills.

What prophets foretold about women in prophesying ministries (preaching, proclaiming God's plan
and His word publicly) will only be fulfilled *as
women see themselves in God's plan and do as Jesus did
in the synagogue; take the prophetic scriptures which they
know apply to them, and assert, proclaim and act upon
them in public ministry. Prophecies must be acted upon
by those who believe them*

That is why Dr. Daisy is active in public ministry
around the world. That is why she is internationally
famous for taking the lead and for using her influence to encourage and to challenge every woman in
Christ to discover her equality, her dignity and her
destiny as a redeemed daughter in God's Royal
Household.

Dr. Daisy believes that those prophecies about
God's *daughters* and about His *handmaidens* reveal
His divine will and desire for women, but that they
will only be fulfilled as women are taught these facts
and as they are challenged to step forth in faith, to
embrace God's will for their lives, and to act upon
His word for them.

Jesus said in Luke 24:44, *that all things MUST BE
FULFILLED, which were written in the LAW of Moses,
in the PROPHETS, and in the PSALMS, CONCERN-
ING ME.* He knew the scriptures *concerning Himself.*
He embraced them and He acted upon them. That is
how they were fulfilled. That is the only way that

prophecies concerning YOU as a woman, can be ful-filled

Dr. Daisy and I want to encourage and to challenge you as a woman, to do as Jesus did: *Know the scriptures concerning YOURSELF.* Embrace them and commit your life to act upon them. In that way, they will be fulfilled in YOU.

The Books of Moses, the Psalms and the Prophets all foretold the coming of Christ. But these prophe-cies were not fulfilled until Jesus *discovered Himself in the scriptures and gave Himself to their fulfillment.* At the very outset of His public ministry, He went into the synagogue and read from Isaiah 61 a prophecy which He believed concerned *Him and His ministry.* (See Luke 4:18).

Throughout Christ's ministry, He acted to fulfill prophecies. Sixteen times, Matthew alone records how Jesus fulfilled the scriptures. And remember that among the religious echelons of society, He was persecuted, condemned and finally killed because He believed those prophecies of the scriptures enough to commit His life to them and to act upon them publicly. He could say, *Lo, I come (in the volume of the book it is written of ME), to do thy will, O God.* Heb. 10:7, Jn. 6:38.

The will or plan of God was uttered by holy pro-phets. Jesus read it, believed it and gave His life to act upon it — *and thus it was fulfilled.*

This is the way Paul discovered redemption for Gentiles the same as for Jews. He found it prophesied in the scriptures, and he gave himself to proclaim it, despite religious opposition that finally cost him His life. But the scriptures of the prophets, foretelling salvation for *whosoever* (Jew or Gentile), were fulfilled *because Paul discovered them, proclaimed them and acted upon them publicly.*

* * *

PART 4

WOMEN FULFILLING PROPHECY

THE PROPHECIES OF Joel, and of others, concerning women in public ministries *in the last days,* will not come to pass by themselves. *They will only be fulfilled when believing women discover the truth of equality in God's redemptive plan* (just as the Gentiles had to do), *and embrace those prophecies of scriptures for themselves, and commit their lives to publicly proclaim and to act upon those scriptures — cost whatever it may cost in religious resistance, opposition or even persecution.*

Women Distinguished By Action

That is what women did in the Early Church. They *acted.*

That is what believing women have done down through the centuries of Church History — though the record of their bravery, of their often extra-ordinary ministries, and of their accomplishments has been scrupulously minimized.

That is what the co-founder of the Salvation Army, Commander Evangeline C. Booth did, despite every cynical and demeaning act or deed that was ever hurled against her brave and gallant leadership of a worldwide ministry of compassion.

That is what Maria Woodworth-Etter did, despite religious and cultural opposition that organized whole packs of male theologians and businessmen in concerted and menacing demonstrations against her massive public healing and miracle meetings across the nation.

That is what Aimee Semple McPhereson did, despite the wholesale opposition of the religious hierarchy, yet she led millions of souls to Christ.

Dr. Daisy's Commitment

That is what Dr. Daisy, my wife and team mate has done in our ministry to millions in over 70 nations. She is literate. She can think. She has a vast library. She has informed herself. She has discovered that God has expressed Himself in the scriptures about His *daughters* and His *handmaidens, in the last days.*

These are the last days. Dr. Daisy is a woman. Long ago, she made a decision that *those prophecies concern her.* She quotes Hebrews 10:7 as her own position: *Then said I, Lo, I come (in the volume of the book it is written of ME* — Daisy Marie Washburn Osborn,) *to do thy will, O God.* He. 10:7 Thus, these prophecies are being fulfilled in Daisy's generation, because they are being fulfilled *through her.* She sees *herself* in these scriptures, and *she is acting upon them.*

That is the essence of what motivates this book. Every feminine member of Christ's body today, who discovers herself in God's redemptive plan revealed in the scriptures, can rise from insignificance and subservient mediocrity (if she chooses), to be numbered among the Royal Daughters of His Divine Family — *Women And Self-Esteem.*

As I said earlier, if I were a woman, I would not permit myself, or my status, or my ministry as a woman to be demeaned or depreciated to a subservient level by the traditions and dictums of male clergymen. I would embrace the scriptures which I believe concern me, exactly as Jesus did, and I would commit my life to carrying out God's will among people.

* * *

PART 5

THE MAKING OF
WOMEN AND SELF-ESTEEM

IN THE BEGINNING, God created man in His own image ... male and female created He them.[Ge.1:27]

From the dawn of human history, God's ideal was a man and a woman, side by side; sharing with each other, working and living together, loving and playing together — companionship, teamwork, intimacy, comradery, partnership. God never created womankind to be the slave or the servant of mankind.

Marriage is the happy state of one woman and one man sharing life together in love and in mutual respect. That was God's original and beautiful dream.

Adam and Eve esteemed each other. They were one flesh, one kind of being. But they disobeyed God and were consequently driven from the garden of Eden because they could no longer live in God's presence after they had sinned. They became the slaves of Satan whom they chose to obey, and their troubles began.

The Problem

Lust began to replace love. Greed and evil superseded good. Because of man's fallen nature and his larger physique, he subjugated woman for his own purposes. Instead of loving her as his own flesh, he manipulated her for monetary advantage and for his physical pleasure.

Deterioration and death resulted and were inbred into all succeeding generations. *The wages of sin is death.*[Ro.6:23] *As by one person, sin entered into the world, and death by sin; so death passed upon all persons, for all have sinned.*[Ro.5:12]

Theology blames womankind for the fall of humanity because Eve was first to partake of the forbidden fruit. But it could be argued as well that Adam disobeyed God before Eve did by allowing Satan to enter the garden which God told him not only to *dress, or to till,* but also to *keep.*[Ge.2:15] (Hebrew: To hedge, to guard, to protect.) Adam was given dominion over Eden but he neglected to exercise his rights — and Satan entered.

Responding to Satan's ruse, *the woman saw that the tree was good ... she took of the fruit thereof, and did eat.* Then the Bible adds, *and Eve gave also to her husband with her; and he did eat, and the eyes of them both were opened.*[Ge.3:6-7] Adam who was *with her,* also did eat. So, not only did Adam neglect to *keep* the garden; he also ate of the forbidden fruit *with* Eve.

It is prejudicial to incriminate Eve and to blame womankind for this original sin, when Adam committed the same transgression. And we must remember that there is also another woman, Mary, whom we can acclaim for our salvation from sin. It was through Mary's obedience that the Savior of the world was born.[Mt.1:2;1; Lu.1:28-38] So if we blame a woman, Eve, for the deterioration of humankind, let us acclaim a woman, Mary, for the redemption of humankind.

If I were a woman, I would no longer see myself as demeaned because of a woman's disobedience. Rather, I would see myself as redeemed because of a woman's obedience.

The Restoration

Thank God, redemption was provided for both womankind and for mankind.[1Pe.2:24] Both have been justified and restored to God through Christ's death and sacrifice in which He endured the judgment of all sins[Ro.5:6; 2Co.5:21] — those of women as well as those of men.

Womankind, as well as mankind, was restored to God to share His life, to do His work and to be His instrument, without social, racial or sexual distinction. On the cross, Jesus abolished female subservience forever.[Ep.2:15-19] But women often still bear the stigma of inferiority because theologians have not emphasized the fact that Christ's redemption restored womankind to her original place with God, the same as mankind was restored.

Two thousand years ago, Jesus liberated every believing woman and man. But outdated church tradition still holds womankind responsible for the fall of humanity, and forbids them to preach or to teach.

This restriction is based on a few remarks made by Paul [1Co.14:34; 1Ti.2:11-12] which are as inapplicable today as it would be to require church members to sell their possessions because they did it in the primitive church. [Ac.4:34-35; 5:1]

Since humanity has been redeemed, Paul says, *We are no longer Jews or Greeks or slaves or free or even men or women, but we are all the same — we are Christians; we are one in Christ Jesus.* [Ga.3:28 LB]

If I were a woman, I would embrace my total salvation and never again acquiesce before any doctrine or teaching or cultural tradition which impugns me or which diminishes my worthiness as Christ's witness, as His representative, as His ambassador or as His co-worker in any private or public ministry to which He calls me.

* * *

PART 6

THE WOMAN PACESETTER

IS IT SIGNIFICANT to you as a woman believer that Mary Magdalene was commissioned by Christ *to find the disciples and to tell them, I have seen the Lord!* Is it significant that *she gave them His message?* [Jn.20:17-18 LB]

It should be encouraging to women believers that

Mary Magdalene was there when Christ arose. He had told His followers that He would rise, but the men were not there. Mary went to the sepulcher, and as a result, she visited with her risen Lord and was chosen by Him to be the first messenger of His resurrection.

And remember: The resurrection is the heartbeat of Christianity. *If Christ be not raised, your faith is vain; you are yet in your sins.*[1Co.15:17] The salvation of every person is linked to the belief and confession *that God has raised Jesus from the dead.*[Ro.10:9]

Jesus said to Mary: *Go to My brethren, and say to them, I ascend to My Father, and your Father; and to My God, and your God.*[Jn.20:17] He sent a woman to proclaim the most vital message of God's redemptive work, to the apostles themselves.

If I were a woman, I would comprehend, by that action, that the ministry of winning souls, of witnessing for Christ and of proclaiming His message is as much for women as it is for men.

* * *

PART 7

THE SPIRIT FILLED WOMAN

THE POWER OF THE Holy Spirit was poured out upon the early believers — both men and women together. Christ said to His followers, *You shall receive power after the Holy Spirit comes upon you and you shall be My witnesses ... to the end of the earth.*[Ac.1:8] Did that promise include women believers?

Jesus used the word *witness,* in a culture where, under Judaism, women were forbidden from any court of law, and were inadmissible as witnesses. Yet, having redeemed and restored them to God, Jesus qualified women forever, as *His witnesses* anywhere on earth.

If women should not be witnesses of Christ's resurrection, why should they have been included in the account? *These all continued with one accord,* in *prayer and supplication, with the women.*[Ac.1:14]

The women were there on the day of Pentecost. The women as well as the men received the Holy Spirit.

Considering the suppressed state of womanhood under Judaism, it is no accident that the Holy Spirit specifies, *with the women ... and they were all filled* so that they could all be *Christ's witnesses,* sharing His good news with the world.

Why was the Holy Spirit given to the women? To be My *witnesses,*[Ac.1:8] Jesus said. The word He used can mean to preach, to teach, to tell, to speak, to prophesy, to demonstrate, to work miracles, to give proof of His resurrection in the form of testimony or of evidence.

Were the men filled with the Holy Spirit to go forth and to preach the gospel with power? Were the women filled with the same Holy Spirit to stay in the house and to be silent?

If I were a woman, I would conclude that the power of the Holy Spirit in my life is to make me an effective *witness* for Christ in any way that He might lead or inspire or call me in private or public ministry.

I do not mean that I would practice leaving behind my household, my husband, or my children to carry the gospel abroad (although men and fathers have done this, without hesitation and without the slightest thought of neglect or desertion, for centuries).

I mean that, if I were a woman, I would respond to God's inspiration or guidance or calling upon my life, with the same confidence and authority that any man is expected to possess (resolving equitably with my spouse, any family problems or challenges or responsibilities which might be involved).

If I were a woman, I would resolve to never allow ecclesiasticisms, dogmas or doctrines to smother, to stifle or to suppress the calling of God and the anointing of the Holy Spirit in my life as Christ's representative and as His *witness*.

* * *

PART 8

THE COMMISSIONED WOMAN

JESUS COMMANDED, *Go to all the world and preach the gospel to every creature.*^{Mk.16:15} Was that command intended for believers of all races, all colors, both sexes?

He said, *These signs shall follow them that believe.*^{Mk.16:17} Did that include Christ's female disciples the same as it did His male disciples?

Jesus said, *Those who believe on Me, the works that I do shall they do also.*^{Jn.14:12} Did that include women believers as well as men believers?

When you understand the subjugation of womankind before redemption, you see why the Bible specifies that the men were *with the women* when the Holy Spirit came.

This experience electrified the community. Crowds from many nations assembled to witness this strange event in Jerusalem. It astounded and shocked them that *the women* were in the midst of it all.

The Prophecy Fulfilled

Peter explained that this was the fulfillment of a major prophecy. He said in essence: *Look, we are not drunk as some of you suppose; this is the fulfillment of Joel's prophecy, I will pour out My Spirit upon all flesh: Your sons and your daughters shall prophesy.*[Ac.2:15-17]

Then Peter continued to quote: *And on My menservants and on My maidservants I will pour out My Spirit in those days and they shall prophesy.*[Ac.2:18]

Peter's explanation: *Jewish tradition has discriminated against women. You marvel that the women are receiving the same power as the men. Your own prophet Joel, said this would happen. He predicted that God would pour out His Spirit upon all flesh; that His sons, His daughters, His servants and His handmaidens would receive power and would prophecy.*

A new day had begun. Womankind had been restored to God the same as mankind, and they recognized their equality as authorized *witnesses* of Christ and as anointed proclaimers of the gospel.

Believers were added to the Lord, multitudes both of men and women.[Ac.5:14]

At that time there was a great persecution against the church ... and they who were scattered abroad went everywhere preaching the word.[Ac.8:1,4]

Both *men and women* were active in *preaching the word.* *Saul* (the great persecutor of those who pro-

240

claimed Christ) *was like a wild man, going everywhere to devastate the believers, even entering private homes and dragging out men and women, and jailing them.*^{Ac.8:3} ^{LB} Would Saul have arrested the women, had they not been spreading Christ's message too?

If I were a woman, I would resolve to exercise every ministry with which Christ would anoint and inspire me, to be part of spreading His message of good news to needy people.

* * *

PART 9

THE ISSUE OF EQUALITY

ALTHOUGH EARLY CHRISTIANS came to realize that Christ's redemption lifted them from primitive racial and sexual discrimination, when the new believers began to organize their communities, delicate and painful issues began to surface.

The new liberty and equality amidst the early believers were tested not only by the seating arrangement, but by many procedures in their new meeting places, where they were still being influenced by Jewish class and gender distinctions.

There were six separate courts in the Jewish Temple: 1) The Court of Gentiles or foreigners, on the outside; 2) the Sacred Enclosure where no Gentile could enter without the penalty of death; 3) the restricted Court of Women; 4) the Court of Israel for male Jews; 5) the Court restricted to Priests; and 6) the House of God.

End of Sex Discrimination

In redemption, all partitions were eliminated. Every believer, regardless of race, sex or other distinction, stood on equal ground before God and could come into His holy presence; all divisions were obliterated between Jews and Gentiles,[Ro.10:12] between men and women,[Ga.3:28] and between priests and the laity.[Re.1:6]

But it was not easy for those Jewish male believers to accept this new equality of womankind

Though they believed that Jesus was the Messiah, they clung to many *traditions, teaching for doctrines the commandments of men.*[Mk.7:7-8; Ti.1:14]

Some refused certain meats.[Ac.10:14; Ac.11:8-9; Ac.15:29; 1Co.8:4-7; 1Ti.4:3-4] Others practiced circumcision.[Ac.15:1-3; Ga.6:12-13] And the matter of women inside the church was, for them, a new situation which they found very difficult to accept.

The Persistent Conflict

There had always been a restricted Women's Court. The men had always been the ones who occupied the principal section. Only males had been permitted to officiate in spiritual worship, to conduct meetings, to debate and to discuss current issues, business affairs, community problems, or to officiate in ceremonies. (In many countries women are still segregated in the public worship services.)

In these new Christian communities, male Jews who had become believers in Christ, grudgingly conceded their superiority over women. It strained their traditional concept of male prominence in God's house for them to admit women into the sanctuary. But the idea of women speaking publicly, or teaching, was simply not acceptable. They rationalized that male superiority should never be expected to sustain such an indignity as that would impose.

Gentile women were never tolerated closer to the Temple than in the Court of the Gentiles — outside the actual Temple. Jewish women had always been restricted within the Women's Court. But now, Jewish — and even Gentile women were permitted inside the sanctuary to see, to hear and even to participate in the worship — something which seemed to many male Jewish believers to be intolerable or even sacrilegious.

But this new status in Christ was intriguing to the women, many of whom were outspoken, or boisterous, or just curious. The fact of male/female equality in these new communities strained their spiritual understanding of Christ's redemption to the point of precipitating agonizing debates and heart-searching *spiritual* double-talk.

But has not the modern world progressed beyond such archaic scruples?

* * *

PART 10

THE NEW GENERATION

IN TODAY'S SOCIETY, does church discipline require Christian hosts to wash a traveler's feet, because it was the custom in Bible days? Do the guardians of church tradition earn their living *by the sweat of their face,*[Ge.3:19] as God said, or do they enjoy air conditioning?

Can sophisticated, educated, Christian women today continue to acquiesce in subservient roles of ministry, and remain silent about giving God's message to the world? In what other areas of society would modern women submit to primitive traditions imposed by antique religious dogmas which oblige them to conform to the customs of past centuries?

The Cost of Silence

The commission of Christ is to share the good news with *every creature*. Women represent two-thirds (if not more) of the body of Christ. More millions would hear the gospel if women who prepare themselves and who desire to obey Christ's call, would become active as public witnesses of Christ and as proclaimers of His gospel.

Why should the traditional church insist upon a doctrine that sequesters Christian women and restrains them from public ministry about Christ, based on two or three cloistered statements made concerning women of an ancient culture? [1Co.14:34; 1Ti.2:11-12]

Prominent scholars agree that the application of these verses to women of all times would contradict Paul's own revelation of redemption.

The *profound* church father, Tertullian, pontificated: *No woman is allowed to speak in church, or even to teach, to baptise or to discharge any man's function, much less to take upon herself the priestly office.*

But Peter said, *You* (meaning women the same as men) *are ... a royal priesthood.*[1Pe.2:9] And John adds, *Jesus Christ has made us* (women as well as men) *kings and priests to God.*[Re.1:6;5:10]

Should church disciplinarians continue to insist upon the discrimination of women, restricting them from public ministry?

Is it not more important to the church that all believers — male and female, become active witnesses, confessors, testifiers or proclaimers of the good news to *every creature* and by every means possible, without restraint based on gender?

To maintain this quaint custom of ministerial discrimination against women believers in the church today — a custom inappropriate to modern society, seems prejudicial to me.

Millions of Moslem women, by their own religious culture, can only be addressed by a woman.

If I were a woman, I would embrace the good news that any redeemed woman has Christ's authority to be His witness, His co-worker, and His messenger anywhere and to anyone, privately or publicly — *to the uttermost part of the earth.*[Ac.1:8]

The Winning Woman

In progressive societies, women and men are educated equally. Women are as accomplished and as professional in the fields of business, of science, of medicine, of education and of politics as men are. Nations are governed by women. Some of the largest business institutions on earth are created, owned and/or presided over by women.

Women had a great share in God's work throughout the Bible, despite being bought and sold like human chattel, restricted from the place of worship, and generally deprived of education. Yet many of them took their places in history among the heroes of all times

The conquests of believing women have been included in countless Biblical and historical documents despite the prejudicial scrutiny of male scribes who flinched at the mention of their gallantry and of their courage. Imagine the undocumented and the untold triumphs of women of Bible times, whose exploits shall never be known, because chauvinistic scribes could not bring themselves to record them for posterity.

The Encouragement

There is a sufficient record preserved in the Bible, and in church history, to motivate and to encourage any woman today who believes in the redemption of Christ for her own life.

The last person at the cross where Christ was crucified was a woman.[Mk.15:47]

The first person at the tomb of Jesus was a woman.[Jn.20:1]

The first person to proclaim the message of our Lord's resurrection was a woman.[Mt.28:8]

The first person to share the gospel with the Jews was a woman.[Lu.2:37-38]

Among those who attended the first recorded prayer meeting after Christ's resurrection were women.[Ac.1:14]

Among the first to be endued with the power of the Holy Spirit, as witnesses for Christ, were women.[Ac.2:4, Ac.1:8]

The first persons to greet the Christian missionaries in Europe — Paul and Silas — were women.
Ac.16:13

The first European convert to believe on Christ
was a woman.Ac.16:14

* * *

PART II

LIMITATIONS OR FREEDOM

WHAT LIMITS ARE appropriate for women in
Christian ministry today?

Contemporary tradition conveniently approves a
woman teaching a Sunday School class, or witnessing in a subdued way of what Christ has done for
her. She may be a missionary, or minister in a house.
She may prepare the food and serve tables at church
affairs (although the men did this in the early
church).Ac.6:2-3

Why should a believing woman be forbidden to
publicly preach or to teach the gospel of Jesus Christ
as His living witness?

If a woman can go to a supermarket, to a park, to a
store or to a sidewalk and witness of Christ, may she
quote scriptures to corroborate her witness? If so,
how many Bible verses may she cite before her witness would be considered to be *preaching* or *teaching*?

If she may witness to one unconverted person, may she witness to two, or to ten, or to a hundred, or to a thousand at the same time? At what point does the number of her listeners exceed the limit for a woman and oblige her to call for a man to do the speaking?

If she may witness to an unconverted person in a subway or in a private house, may she witness to one or to many in a public hall which she might rent, or under a tent which she might erect?

If she may witness along a footpath or a side-walk, suppose a group gathers. May she step up on a boulder, or a box or a chair in order to be heard? Could she mount a platform? How loud may she speak before she is out of order?

If she may pray for one unbeliever, may she pray for two, or ten, or a hundred at a time? How many is too many for a woman?

If she may witness, may she teach or preach?

Should modern Christian women submit to the restraints of antiquated cultural sex discrimination which denies them equality in public ministry for Christ? If I were a woman, I would not.

Do believing women have the Biblical right to allow their witness for Christ to be suppressed? Can they surrender to silence in Christian ministry because of Paul's statements, when so many scholars agree that his remarks have been taken out of their cultural context, misconstrued, and unjustly applied to women of this epoch?

If I were a woman, I would not surrender to the repression of my ministry. If someone told me that I could not publicly teach or preach about Jesus, I would thank God for my voice and for my right of choice to obey my Lord as His witness, despite the demeaning ruse of supressionists in the church.

The Field — The World

Informed women know that the only area where they have been forbidden to *teach* and to *speak* is inside the church buildings.[1Co.14:34] (The Greek word which Paul used means *a religious congregation, assembly, Jewish synagogue, etc.*)

Even if women acquiesce to this primitive restraint inside the churches, there is no scriptural limits on the ministry of a Christian woman outside the church walls. That is where sharing the good news is most needed and most effective.

Daisy asks: *Why should women feel discouraged in their ministries when restricted to silence inside the church building? The world is our field,* Jesus said. [Mt.13:38]

She advises: *Rather than to publicly remain silent about Christ and His love, let believing women lift up their eyes and look on the fields* [Jn.4:35] *of the whole world, out where they can obey their Lord without contravening theological scruples about women.*

If women submit to what Paul is alleged to have taught about being silent inside the church building, let them obey what Christ clearly taught about being His witness outside the church — *to the end of the earth.*[Ac.1:8] I heartily agree with Daisy.

It is not wrong for believing women to go out where the people are, to give Christ's message to the world, privately or publicly, and to win souls to Him

There is a new army of spiritual Joans of Arc who recognize their freedom and their equality in redemption. They are on the rise, worldwide, and they are giving the good news to millions throughout the world who might not be reached without the ministry of these courageous believing women. This is progress in Christian ministry.

The Female Awakening

Should we not *rightly divide the word of truth?* [2Ti.2:15] Should educated Christian women acquiesce to sex discrimination in God's work and bow to religious subservience because of Paul's words which have been misconstrued to imply a contradiction of all of his own revelation and teaching about the redemption of womankind the same as mankind?

Are scriptures to be qualified sexually? Are the class and sex distinctions of archaic Bible cultures to be imposed today? Only upon the women? Was the redemption of womankind limited? Was she redeemed, but kept at a distance? Is she justified before God, but considered *unqualified* to speak for Christ who restored her? Were her sins forgiven? Forgotten by God? But remembered by men? — while the sins of mankind were expunged forever?

The Believing Woman

Should a woman who believes in redemption, and who desires to share the good news, allow men or systems to forbid her from doing what Jesus commissioned her to do?

Can believing women afford to permit persons, or boards, or institutions to limit or to stifle their witness for Christ who chose a woman to proclaim the greatest message in Christianity — that He is risen?

Are Christian women to be silent in God's work today when so many women in the Bible were His messengers?

Is it possible for a believing woman to use Paul's words as an excuse for her own lack of courage to become involved in giving Christ's message to the world?

Can believing women afford to bow to discrimination in the church world, while in the secular world their equality is a fact of life?

Should Christian women be considered inferior or subservient in the church, while their equality is evidenced in business, in science, in medicine, in politics and in government? Should primitive sex-discrimination be imposed only upon the women in today's church? Is any such cultural yoke imposed upon Christian men today?

* * *

PART 12

THE WOMAN I WOULD BE

THESE ARE SOME of the positions that I would assume, with all sincerity and due respect for anyone who might seek to restrain or to limit me — if I were a woman believer in the family of God.

1. If I were a woman, I would obey Jesus Christ outside the church building — if I felt led or inspired or called to do so, as much as I would tolerate religious tradition inside the church institution.

2. If I were a woman, I would consider myself a Christian, a believer, a follower of Christ, His *witness* and a messenger of His resurrection to *every creature,* to any extent to which I felt led or inspired to act.

3. If I were a woman, I would embrace the fact that Christ lives in me, He serves through me, He speaks through me, He loves and ministers through me; that my body is His body; that He is free to continue His same ministry through me that He exercised in

Bible times; that *as God sent Christ into the world, even so Christ sends me into the world.*[Jn.17:18; 20:21 Paraphrased]

4. If I were a woman, I would do what Christ told believers to do even if I was criticized or misjudged for doing it. Christ suffered reproach for me. *The servant is not above his or her Master.*[Mt.10:24]

5. If I were a woman, I would be one of the wise persons *who heard the sayings of Christ and did them,*[Mt.7:24] building my ministry as His witness upon the rock of faith and action.

6. If I were a woman, filled with the Holy Spirit, I would be Christ's *witness in Jerusalem, in all Judea, in Samaria, and to the end of the earth*[Ac.1:8] to any extent that I felt His call or guidance.

7. If I were a woman and felt God's call to do so, I would act on Joel's prophecy: *I will pour out My spirit upon all flesh; and your sons and your daughters shall prophesy.*[Jl.2:28] I would observe that Peter quoted that prophecy: *On My menservants and on My handmaidens will I pour out of My spirit; and they shall prophesy.*[Ac.2:18] I would be glad that the Hebrew word used by Joel means: Speak or sing by inspiration; to predict or to give a discourse; and that the Greek word used by Peter means: To speak under divine inspiration; to exercise a prophetic office; an inspired speaker.

8. If I were a woman, I would note that Jesus never made a difference between the sexes. I would be impressed by the different women who were associated

with His life and ministry. If I felt the desire or call to do so, I would be like the woman of Samaria who, as soon as she believed, evangelized a whole city for Jesus. *The people went out of the city and came to Him ... and many of the Samaritans of the city believed on Him* [Jn.4:39] because of the testimony and the ministry of a woman.

9. If I were a woman, I would remember: 1) that Jesus is my Lord — not Paul or any of the church fathers; 2) that Jesus commissioned women followers (as well as men followers) to *preach the gospel* years before Paul was even converted; 3) that the Holy Spirit endowed women believers (as well as men believers) with *power* to be Christ's *witnesses*, years before Paul even believed on Christ; 4) that Jesus Christ, my Savior and Lord, is the one who saved me, empowered me, and called me — not Paul; and 5) that any private or public ministry I might engage in, or any claim of authority to preach or to teach the gospel which I might express is not dependent upon theological tradition, church dogma, or ecclesiastical endorsement, but is based upon the teachings and the commission of my own Lord Jesus Christ, *whom I belong to and whom I serve.* [Ac.27:23]

10. If I were a woman, I would recognize the full redemptive work of God's grace on my behalf, through Christ; I would embrace my identity as a believer in Christ, redeemed through His shed blood, with all of the inherited rights, privileges and responsibilities of any member, male or female, of

God's royal family; and I would never allow any voice, edict, dogma, rule, or doctrine to limit the exercise of my authority as Christ's *witness*, private or public, or to repress my Christian ministry to people anywhere.

The Status — The Message

Jesus commissions women and men alike to go out where the people are, to the busy boulevards and crossroads of society, out in public halls, theaters, cinemas, parks and ball fields, in houses and mobile homes, under trees, tents, arbors or roofs, to tell the world, *I have seen the Lord* and to give *them His message!* Jn.20:18 LB

That is what I would do if I were a woman — one who desires to share Jesus Christ with all those for whom He died.

VIII

CREATED
FOR
HONOR

A WOMAN SEARCHES to justify her inner awakening. As a female she is created with an inborn sensitivity toward people.

What is happening today cannot be ignored. It will not go away. Therefore, it is time to understand its origin and to reappraise primitive attitudes.

In her quest for personal identity, it is imperative that a woman discover God. There will be no discovering of her true *Self-Esteem* without the recognition of her legitimate origin in God.

I believe the Bible is true. I have committed my life to the principle that the Bible is God's word. A woman can trust it, and its balanced message is the one sure formula that assures the feminine gender a sure place among God's valued company of *Women And Self-Esteem*.

Womankind is a creation of God and is made in His image. He is our Father. We are His daughters. He cares very much about each detail of a woman's life. He is aware of every wound or embarrassment she has ever sustained.

Never allow any person, system, influence, dogma, doctrine or society to cause you to forget that *you* are *Created For Honor*, nor that *you* are a distinguished and a vital member of God's regal lineage of *Women And Self-Esteem*.

Chapter 8

CREATED FOR HONOR

A WOMAN SEARCHES to justify her inner awakening. As a female she is created with an inborn sensitivity toward people.

The woman God created in His own image is inclined to gentleness. She desires honesty. She is practiced in strategy.

As her stirring intensifies, a woman will discover that her deep desire for originality and for personal identity is rooted in the truth of her origin. It is fundamental to the realization of her God-given potential.

Natural — Divine — Prophetic

I am convinced, after much research, study and prayer, that the life of Jesus Christ reflects God's desire, God's ideal and God's plan for the finest development of all human persons — including those He created in female form. *Women And Self-Esteem* has been His design from the beginning.

Religionists tend to placate and appease the female who questions her traditional slot in society and in religion. This method has repressed and tranquilized women from the earliest epochs of religious history.

However, there is an awakening taking place now in every nation of the world that is not the result of a social, economic or political movement. It is the vital fulfillment of prophecy concerning this epoch prior to the return of Jesus Christ.

What is happening today cannot be ignored. It will not go away. Therefore, it is best to understand its origin and to reappraise primitive attitudes. This is an opportunity to learn, to grow and to improve society, rather than to obstruct prophetic fulfillment.[Jl. 2:28]

Religious Roots

The universal male-female inequity has its roots in religion.

I can say this because of the fact that God created humankind — female and male — equal, in His own image and just a little lower than Himself.[Ge. 1:27; Ge. 5:2]

God did not create religion. God and religion are not synonymous, nor are they compatible.

Religion Versus God

God never changes.

Religion does change to accommodate social trends and contemporary prejudices. Since men usually direct such change, the male stands to gain from these rules of order and legislation without equalization.

The wealthy, the learned, the white and the male, stand out in history as the directors of thought, the enforcers of submission, the practicers of slavery, and the segregators of human persons.

I say this to underscore the fact that God and religion are not synonymous.

Religion is not all bad. But God is only good.

Religion has its limits. God has no limits.

Religion accentuates the weakness of people — especially the female. God only enhances the greatness, the excellence and the dignity of all individuals — female and male.

Religion places obstacles to personal development and to individual initiative and performance — especially for the female. God makes us know that we can do anything regardless of our sex. [Mk 9:23]

Religion proposes a chain of command, an order of protocol. Jesus, who came as God in the flesh, could be approached openly by anyone — even a woman.[Mk 5:24-34] He came to show us God's attitude toward each of us — the female and the male. He used such words as: *Any, everyone, all,* and *whoever, etc.*

Religion is usually too biased against women to approve the freedom of their creative thought and initiative. But God's ingenuity can be expressed through any person who is free to dream, to discover and to achieve.

Where Can A Woman Begin?

In her quest for personal identity and self-dignity, it is imperative that a woman discover God. There will be no discovering of her true self-esteem without her recognition of her legitimate origin in God.

The starting point for a woman's search must, therefore, be the Bible. I believe that the Bible is true and that it is the word of God.

Here are five basic non-theological reasons for believing the Bible.

1. THE CONTENT OF THE BIBLE. The Bible's total harmony and coherency are too miraculous to be coincidental.

Forty different authors wrote sixty-six books spanning almost two thousand years. They were scattered across two continents and almost none of them were ever known or contacted by the others. But the cohesion of truth, the principles of faith and the story of redemption about which they wrote are synonymous.

Common sense tells me that the Bible is inspired by a Master-Designer.

2. THE WITNESS OF MARTYRS. Many good, honest people have believed in the truths of the Bible and in its teachings and principles.

Many of them endured unbelievable torture, suffering and death itself for the testimony of their faith. History records the sacrifice of many thousands of such gallant women and men. They died in love, not in revenge or anger.

This impresses me to believe in what the martyrs died for much more than I could believe in those who killed them.

3. THE PEOPLE I HAVE KNOWN. The people who taught me Bible-based truths and principles were the upright, honorable and respected women and men in the community.

They only wanted my good, I could trust them. Their faith produced the kind of life I wanted.

I trust what they taught more than I could ever trust those who deny the Bible.

4. THE LIFE OF JESUS. The accounts of Jesus

Christ's life show that He was good, kind and compassionate.

He healed, blessed and lifted people. He never condemned or berated human persons.

He quoted the scripture as God's word. He taught it. He believed it.

He advocated the greatest principles ever enunciated by any leader. Everything He taught was confirmed by miracles, signs and wonders. No one ever convinced Him of prejudice, of dishonesty or of demoralization of human beings.

I trust Jesus more than any leader, statesman, author or philosopher who denies that He is God's Son.

5. THE RESURRECTION OF JESUS. History is replete with the testimonies of honorable women and men who say they saw the Lord Jesus after He had been publicly crucified.

From the days of the early church when as many as 500 people say that they saw Christ at one time, to this century, thousands of people have given the same witness.

He has appeared to both me and to my husband individually. I have no reason to lie.

In almost every crusade that my husband and I have conducted, in over 70 nations, people have said that they saw the Lord Jesus alive. Would

Hindus, Moslems, Buddhists, Shintoists or atheists lie about seeing Jesus? Over 100 Buddhists saw Him at one time in our Thailand Crusade.

I believe the Bible is true. I have committed my life to the principle that the Bible is God's word and that it is true. A woman can trust it, and she has not only the right, but also the duty, as a believer, to proclaim it.

Female Followers

The Bible tells us that Jesus had multitudes of female and male disciples or followers.

They talked with Him and learned from Him. They witnessed His life, His teaching and His miracles. They were constantly amazed by His words and His actions.

Whether or not His first disciples fully comprehended that Jesus was God in the form of a human, we cannot know. However, because of their witness of Jesus' life and teachings, a woman can now understand that He was and is precisely that.*Jn.16:28; Jn.10:30; Jn 12:44-50*

After Jesus was crucified and raised from the dead, He appeared first to one of His faithful female followers, Mary Magdalene. Then He said to all of His disciples — both female and male: *As My Father has sent me, in the same way, I send you.*Jn.20:21

Naturally they were shocked. Were they expected to even do miracles like Jesus had done?

Could they show love to every person — female and male, in the same way Jesus had done? Could they possibly touch and lift up the so-called outcasts of religion as He had done?

Yes, they could, because Jesus had said: *When you believe on me, you* (believers — female and male) *will do the same works I have done; and greater works than these will you do because I go to My Father.*[Jn.14:12]

How must the female followers of Jesus have felt when they heard those words?

A Woman's Plight

Traditional religion has almost never endorsed women in functions of public ministry, despite Joel's inspired utterance that, *in the last days,* both *daughters* and *handmaidens* would PROPHECY. (Be sure to read Chapter 7.)

In fact, when Jesus came, the female had been reduced to a restricted, passive, muted, subservient role by religion.

A Jewish woman was not even allowed to study the scriptures, though some rabbis secretly taught their daughters the Torah, violating their own Jewish laws. Perhaps, their love for God and His creation was greater than their love for Rabbinical laws.

In the Talmud, certain rabbis classified the female as a non-freed slave. What was their reasoning?

Slaves had masters and a Jewish woman had her master. She was owned by her father or her husband or some other male member of her family.

Understanding the plight of a woman in the time of Jesus is necessary to the comprehension of what He did to show God's attitude toward His female creation, and toward the rules of the religious men who suppressed them.

The cruelty of religion in Bible times is illustrated by the many categories of human persons who were segregated from holy worship, and were regarded with disdain. The female was included in one of those thought-to-be inferior groups.

Even a sick person, or one who was imperfect or diseased, a blind or lame person, or one who was nearsighted or had crossed eyes, one who had a speech impediment or even a mark on their body, such as a birthmark, was excluded from the holy places.[Le.21:17-24]

The New Meaning of *Master*

It is understandable why a woman called Jesus

Master.*Jn.20:16*

Though we know that this title meant *teacher* or *rabbi* to the Jewish male, as a woman one can be sure that it meant *liberator* to both the Jewish and the Gentile females.

No longer are human persons to be regarded as males or females, slaves or free, Jews or Gentiles; each one is liberated, a re-created daughter or son of God when they accept Jesus Christ into their life. *Ga.3:28; Jn.8:36; Mt.6:24*

A woman has only one Master when she receives Jesus Christ as her savior and Lord.

A woman can know God personally as her heavenly Father and can learn more about His nature, His character. How? By studying the life of Jesus Christ — His words, His ministry, His encounters with people. She should pay special attention to His encounters with women. And it is in His likeness that a woman is made.

I can testify to the excitement and fulfillment that a woman realizes when she discovers the truth that Jesus has revealed about God and His female creation.

The Greatest Teacher

Some of the most classic teachings of Jesus are contained in just five verses of scripture midway in His *Sermon on the Mount*. These well known verses can empower a woman's life only as they become her prayer and her guide in life.

This portion of scripture is called the *Lord's Prayer.*^{Mt.6:9-13} However, it is much more than a prayer. For a woman or a man, a girl or a boy, of any nation or race, at any academic or social level, it is a pattern for thinking, for living and for being.

This prayer contains only 66 words and takes about 20 seconds to recite. Every day it is repeated in hundreds of dialects by more than 500 million people around the world.

But this is not a prayer for a woman to simply recite. This is a prayer to be lived.

When a woman prays the *Lord's Prayer*, it will shape her whole thought pattern. It will form her attitudes and keep her happy and healthy. It will lift her above life's toughest situations, and it will enable her to become all that God created a woman to be.

In the six phrases known as the *Lord's Prayer*, there are seven basic seed-ideas for the woman who wants to live life to its fullest and best.

Negative Forces

Those seven basic seed-ideas contain the answers to the seven most destructive influences which prevent a woman from truly living a winner's life.

These negative forces are:

1. Insignificance, unworthiness, inferiority, lack of value;

2. Despair, dejection, discouragement, despondency;

3. Tension, anxiety, worry, apprehension;

4. Condemnation, shame, humiliation, guilt;

5. Animosity, bitterness, depression, vindictiveness;

6. Distrust, fear, agitation, distress;

7. Ignorance, lack of understanding, unawareness.

If a woman has experienced any of these negative influences in her life, she can conquer them once and for all by praying the *Lord's Prayer.* It is important that she pray with an open mind, a fervent heart, a flexible attitude, an uncluttered spirit and a willingness to change.

Seven Positive Stages Of Change

New information and added knowledge produce change in a woman.

Change is good when it means a better way of living.

How can a woman bring about changes in her life? If she takes one step at a time, change follows a natural evolution.

First, a woman hears truth or receives knowledge that she did not have previously.

Second, a woman accepts this new knowledge and believes it with all of her heart.

Third, she practices an awareness, a consciousness of the knowledge she has gained.

Fourth, she starts taking steps to put what she has learned into action in her life.

Fifth, a woman's lifestyle becomes automated by her new knowledge. She forms new habits.

Sixth, she modifies her relationships in order to enhance her new lifestyle. Nothing stays the same.

Seventh, a woman releases past experiences and the relationships that hamper her personal growth and she develops awareness.

This is an important fact to remember: *All that a woman can take into her future of constant change and development is the knowledge that she has gained from past experiences and former relationships.*

Insignificance

The first destructive emotion that is dealt with in the *Lord's Prayer* is the sense of insignificance or inferiority.

The origin of many negative words can be found in religion. That is because religion practices the evaluation and classification of human persons.

I have personally taught people among most of the major religions of the world. Without exception I have seen human beings slotted into categories by their religious teachers.

There is nothing more demoralizing to a woman's ego than to be considered insignificant, incapable or inferior. To be discriminated against because of one's academic level, social status, race, color, language or sex is debasing and abusive to the divine personhood of a woman or a man.

The opening statement of our Lord's prayer is a confession of a woman's equality before God — and consequently before every other human person.

Behavior — Human Or Inhuman?

There is so much for a woman to learn in the realm of human behavior. The *Lord's Prayer* is a treasure from which she can learn.

I have observed with astounding regularity that most women do exactly what society and culture programs them to do.

Words, whether negative or positive, form a

272

sequence of coded instructions to a woman's sub-conscious. Unaware that it has been given a command, the brain begins to assimilate the messages and the instructions, negative or positive, that will eventually be carried out.

A Chinese woman is programmed by China's culture and religion. She acts out the role for which she is programmed. Africa's culture and religion programs the African woman to act as she does. India's culture and religion programs the Indian woman to act as she does.

Western culture — through educational and social environments, via TV and radio, from the pulpit or theater, through advertisements and publications, programs the Western woman to act out the role dictated to her subconscious mind.

Why does a woman not stop to question whether the mold society pours her into is the lifestyle for which God designed her?

A World Of Women

Over fifty years of attending to the spiritual, physical, mental, emotional and material needs of people in over 70 different nations, has made me highly sensitive to women and extremely aware of their God-given potential.

The hurts, the scars and the insecurities of a woman are of great concern to me, because I know these negative influences demoralize her. They stifle the development of a woman's true potential created in her by God.

Jesus said that there would be injuries, humiliations, abuses, assaults and crimes committed against individuals.[Ro.12:19] It seems that the majority of those *individuals* are women.

The performers of such negative deeds feel a need for revenge. They have been hurt, so they must hurt someone else. The frustration of feeling defenseless or victimized causes one to seek reprisal. But retribution is never the solution. Vengeance is not an action that results in growth.[Mt.18:7]

The first line of the *Lord's Prayer*, if prayed with sincerity, will heal a woman's wounds and make her a healer of the wounds of others.

Jesus takes the things intended to hurt a woman and makes them into something that will help her. So I encourage a woman to reach for the stars; not to treat her scars.

Positive Is Greater Than Negative

A sense of inferiority in a woman expresses itself by demeaning another. A woman's negative attitude toward another person will motivate injury and abuse, and it always indicates a negative attitude toward herself.

The woman who is positive towards another person, and who is an uplifting influence on another, is the woman who feels positive and confident herself.

A feeling of inferiority or insignificance invariably puts another down, minimizing their value or disparaging their virtue.

She Does It To Herself

By rejecting another, a woman rejects herself.

By accepting another, a woman accepts herself.

By criticizing another, a woman criticizes herself.

By valuing another, a woman values herself.

By resenting another, a woman resents herself.

By loving another, a woman loves herself.

An Inferior Woman — NEVER!

There are always superior and inferior performances, but there are never superior or inferior women. Never judge a woman by her performance. Always separate the act from the actor, the deed from the doer.

A woman's performance will improve with practice and development. But whether her deed is clumsy, inferior, unpolished or unheralded, all the while she is a super person, never an inferior one.

It's A Crime

When a woman accepts being inferior, she is committing a crime against herself. She can express this crime in many different ways.

Timidity expresses itself in a woman with physical manifestations that expose a sense of inadequacy.

A common expression of inadequacy in a woman is her difficulty in accepting a compliment.

A woman's sense of insignificance is revealed by embarrassment if she is served by someone else.

The emotion of inferiority is revealed in a woman when she is apologetic in any attempt to state her personal opinion in a matter.

A woman displays a feeling of inadequacy when she is ashamed of an honest mistake, or of an unavoidable delay.

This demoralizing emotion of lack of self esteem in a woman exhibits itself in her self-criticism or in negative, destructive remarks or putdowns made about herself. It can also manifest itself in her delight over the failure of another person.

These are only a few of the outward indications of a woman's inward feeling of inferiority and insignificance.

How can this crime be stamped out of a woman's life?

A Sense Of Pride

It is no wonder that our Lord Jesus began His prayer as He did: *Our Father* ... It was a purposeful reminder to every woman that she is a creation of God. Therefore, she cannot be inferior or insignificant in His eyes.

As a woman have you ever felt unimportant or without significance? Is there a sense of pride when you look around you or do you feel ashamed?

If you have had these thoughts, you are not alone. Nearly every woman deals with inferiority and insignificance sooner or later. That must be why Jesus taught us to begin our prayer to *Our Father in heaven* by recognizing and confessing our identity as His daughter, in His royal family.

A Woman's Real Identity

In other words, begin your prayer by remembering who God is and who you are.

A woman is saying: *God is my Father. I am His daughter. This is my true identity.*

277

My heavenly Father sees me, a woman, as important. I see myself as important. My Father says I, a woman, can do anything. I believe I can do anything.

Our heavenly Father is perfect. He will help the woman who strives to attain this goal.

No one should measure her ability by that of someone else. A woman can constantly elevate her own position in life through improvement. She can break her own records by requiring herself to achieve on a higher level with each accomplishment.

True Family Identity

When a woman prays: *My heavenly Father,* she cannot be inferior or insignificant. Since she is God's daughter, she cannot be of a lower value than another of His daughters or sons.

When a woman prays: *Our Father,* immediately she feels loved, cared for, understood, sheltered, provided for, esteemed, trusted, needed and depended upon.

When she accepts her divine identity, she discovers that she already has a name that is highly honored.

Our Father, means that we are great. We can do anything. We are productive. We are loved. We have the mind of Christ. We have Jesus.

When a woman prays, *Our Father*, that is a confession that she is a creation of God. She is a sister to every other human being on earth. She is a member of the family of humankind.

How can religion suggest that part of God's family is subservient or inferior to the other part? Performance might vary, but individual value and dignity does not. God's daughters and His sons are equal.

A Variety Of Prayers?

When Jesus taught us to pray, *Our Father*, He was teaching a mixed multitude. This one prayer was significant for the entire mass of people whether they were Jews, Gentiles, males, females, slaves or masters.

Jesus did not teach a separate prayer for each social, sexual or religious category.

God classifies humankind just a little lower than Himself.[Ps.8:4-6] That is how a believing woman identifies herself.

Religion introduces the idea that the female person is subordinate, imperfect, deficient, of poor quality and with a low grade of efficiency and therefore must live in subservient submission.

One of the most obvious signs of insignificance in a person is their deprecation of another person.

So, in attempting to brand God's daughters as inferior beings, religionists have exposed their own problem of inferiority.

This act by religious leaders is both self-incriminating and detrimental to human dignity as the creation of God.

You See In Others
What You See In Yourself

As a woman, reflect on your attitude toward others — both women and men alike. Do you make others feel better about themselves? Or do you leave them feeling inferior or insignificant? Your attitude toward others is an indication of how you really feel about yourself.

How do you behave with your spouse? What is your conduct with your parents or your children or other family members? Are you a positive influence in your community? In your church? In the work force? In society?

When a woman resents others, she is resented by others. And when she loves others, she is loved by others.

When a woman thinks that she hates another person, she is really expressing hatred for something deep inside herself. By the same token she can only love another person if she loves herself.

A woman can accept another person as they are

and where they are, to the extent that she can accept herself as she is and where she is. As a woman allows the people around her to grow, to change and to develop, she will experience the same improvement.

Evaluating, assessing or judging another person is not a woman's purpose in life. Jesus was God in the flesh and He said that He did come to judge.[Jn12:47] No one else has the right to evaluate, rule, control, impede, criticize or intimidate another person. That is an attitude which is foreign to a follower of Jesus.

A woman can modify, grow, improve and change herself, by identifying with her heavenly Father. She will then be amazed at how the world around her improves.

Jesus Said: Follow Me

Separate God from religion and follow your teachers only as they follow Jesus Christ.

Study the life and the words and the encounters of the ministry of Jesus Christ. He came to show us God, our heavenly Father.

Begin each conversation with God by saying:

My Father who is in heaven, Your name is holy.

When a woman prays as Jesus taught, she is a woman who is identifying with greatness, with success, with power and with victory. She is a woman *Created For Honor*, the honor of her heavenly Father.

Woman's Daily Confession

I am valuable as a *woman*, because I am created in God's class of being.

I am *vital* as a *woman*, because God's plan involves me.

My *heritage* as a *woman*, is to have God's best, to enjoy His companionship and to use His wealth and power for the good of myself and others.

The seeds of *greatness* are in me — a woman. God never created me to be a *Nobody*, but a real *Somebody*.

Therefore, as a *woman*, I recognize myself as one of God's redeemed *Women And Self-Esteem*. I know that God designed me for His lifestyle and I now know that He planned Life's *best* for me as His child.

As a *woman*, I shall no longer discredit or demean or destroy what God created in His own image and values so much.

I welcome God's friendly voice to me, as a *woman*. He reminds me of my divine origin, of my high purpose, and of His love plan to help me to achieve, to enjoy and to share His blessings in life. Because of His redemption, I have true *Self-Esteem* in Jesus Christ my only Lord and Master.

Signed _____

Sign, this confession, keep it with your Bible, and read it aloud every time anyone or anything tries to demean or to dishearten you. Never allow any person, system, influence, dogma, doctrine or society to cause you to forget that *you* are *Created For Honor,* nor that *you* are a distinguished and a vital member of God's regal lineage of *Women And Self-Esteem.*

WOMEN & SELF-ESTEEM